WILLIAM SHAKESPEARE was born in Stratford-upon-Avon in April 1564, and his birth is traditionally celebrated on April 23. The facts of his life, known from surviving documents, are sparse. He was one of eight children born to John Shakespeare, a merchant of some standing in his community. William probably went to the King's New School in Stratford, but he had no university education. In November 1582, at the age of eighteen, he married Anne Hathaway, eight years his senior, who was pregnant with their first child, Susanna. She was born on May 26, 1583. Twins, a boy, Hamnet (who would die at age eleven), and a girl, Judith, were born in 1585. By 1592 Shakespeare had gone to London, working as an actor and already known as a playwright. A rival dramatist, Robert Greene, referred to him as "an upstart crow, beautified with our feathers." Shakespeare became a principal shareholder and playwright of the successful acting troupe the Lord Chamberlain's men (later, under James I, called the King's men). In 1599 the Lord Chamberlain's men built and occupied the Globe Theatre in Southwark near the Thames River. Here many of Shakespeare's plays were performed by the most famous actors of his time, including Richard Burbage, Will Kempe, and Robert Armin. In addition to his 37 plays, Shakespeare had a hand in others, including *Sir Thomas More* and *The Two Noble Kinsmen*, and he wrote poems, including *Venus and Adonis* and *The Rape of Lucrece*. His 154 sonnets were published, probably without his authorization, in 1609. In 1611 or 1612 he gave up his lodgings in London and devoted more and more of his time to retirement in Stratford, though he continued writing such plays as *The Tempest* and *Henry VIII* until about 1613. He died on April 23, 1616, and was buried in Holy Trinity Church, Stratford. No collected edition of his plays was published during his lifetime, but in 1623 two members of his acting company, John Heminges and Henry Condell, published the great collection now called the First Folio.

**Bantam Shakespeare
The Complete Works—29 Volumes
Edited by David Bevington
With forewords by Joseph Papp on the plays**

The Poems: Venus and Adonis, The Rape of Lucrece, The
Phoenix and Turtle, A Lover's Complaint,
the Sonnets

Antony and Cleopatra	*The Merchant of Venice*
As You Like It	*A Midsummer Night's Dream*
The Comedy of Errors	*Much Ado about Nothing*
Hamlet	*Othello*
Henry IV, Part One	*Richard II*
Henry IV, Part Two	*Richard III*
Henry V	*Romeo and Juliet*
Julius Caesar	*The Taming of the Shrew*
King Lear	*The Tempest*
Macbeth	*Twelfth Night*

Together in one volume:

Henry VI, Parts One, Two, and Three
King John and Henry VIII
*Measure for Measure, All's Well that Ends Well, and
Troilus and Cressida*
Three Early Comedies: Love's Labor's Lost, The Two
Gentlemen of Verona, The Merry
Wives of Windsor
Three Classical Tragedies: Titus Andronicus, Timon
of Athens, Coriolanus
The Late Romances: Pericles, Cymbeline, The Winter's
Tale, The Tempest

Two collections:

Four Comedies: The Taming of the Shrew, A Midsummer
Night's Dream, The Merchant of Venice,
Twelfth Night
Four Tragedies: Hamlet, Othello, King Lear, Macbeth

William Shakespeare

TWELFTH NIGHT
or
WHAT YOU WILL

Edited by
David Bevington

David Scott Kastan,
James Hammersmith,
and Robert Kean Turner,
Associate Editors

With a Foreword by
Joseph Papp

BANTAM BOOKS
TORONTO / NEW YORK / LONDON / SYDNEY / AUCKLAND

TWELFTH NIGHT
*A Bantam Book / published by arrangement
with Scott, Foresman and Company*

PRINTING HISTORY
Scott, Foresman edition published / January 1980
*Bantam edition, with newly edited text and substantially revised,
edited, and amplified notes, introductions, and other
materials, published / February 1988*
*Valuable advice on staging matters has been
provided by Richard Hosley.
Collations checked by Eric Rasmussen.
Additional editorial assistance by Claire McEachern.*

Library of Congress Cataloging-in-Publication Data

Shakespeare, William, 1564–1616.
   Twelfth night / William Shakespeare; edited by David Bevington;
David Scott Kastan, James Hammersmith, and Robert Kean Turner,
associate editors; with a foreword by Joseph Papp.
     p.   cm.—(A Bantam classic)
   "Bantam edition with newly edited text and substantially revised,
edited, and amplified notes, introductions, and other materials"—
—T.p. verso.
   Bibliography: p.
   ISBN 0-553-21308-3 (pbk.)
   I. Bevington, David M. II. Title.
PR2837.A2B38 1988
822.3′3—dc19   87-23193
                                     CIP

Published simultaneously in the United States and Canada

Contents

Foreword

It's hard to imagine, but Shakespeare wrote all of his plays with a quill pen, a goose feather whose hard end had to be sharpened frequently. How many times did he scrape the dull end to a point with his knife, dip it into the inkwell, and bring up, dripping wet, those wonderful words and ideas that are known all over the world?

In the age of word processors, typewriters, and ballpoint pens, we have almost forgotten the meaning of the word "blot." Yet when I went to school, in the 1930s, my classmates and I knew all too well what an inkblot from the metal-tipped pens we used would do to a nice clean page of a test paper, and we groaned whenever a splotch fell across the sheet. Most of us finished the school day with ink-stained fingers; those who were less careful also went home with ink-stained shirts, which were almost impossible to get clean.

When I think about how long it took me to write the simplest composition with a metal-tipped pen and ink, I can only marvel at how many plays Shakespeare scratched out with his goose-feather quill pen, year after year. Imagine him walking down one of the narrow cobblestoned streets of London, or perhaps drinking a pint of beer in his local alehouse. Suddenly his mind catches fire with an idea, or a sentence, or a previously elusive phrase. He is burning with impatience to write it down—but because he doesn't have a ballpoint pen or even a pencil in his pocket, he has to keep the idea in his head until he can get to his quill and parchment.

He rushes back to his lodgings on Silver Street, ignoring the vendors hawking brooms, the coaches clattering by, the piteous wails of beggars and prisoners. Bounding up the stairs, he snatches his quill and starts to write furiously, not even bothering to light a candle against the dusk. "To be, or not to be," he scrawls, "that is the—." But the quill point has gone dull, the letters have fattened out illegibly, and in the middle of writing one of the most famous passages in the history of dramatic literature, Shakespeare has to stop to sharpen his pen.

Taking a deep breath, he lights a candle now that it's dark, sits down, and begins again. By the time the candle has burned out and the noisy apprentices of his French Huguenot landlord have quieted down, Shakespeare has finished Act 3 of *Hamlet* with scarcely a blot.

Early the next morning, he hurries through the fog of a London summer morning to the rooms of his colleague Richard Burbage, the actor for whom the role of Hamlet is being written. He finds Burbage asleep and snoring loudly, sprawled across his straw mattress. Not only had the actor performed in *Henry V* the previous afternoon, but he had then gone out carousing all night with some friends who had come to the performance.

Shakespeare shakes his friend awake, until, bleary-eyed, Burbage sits up in his bed. "Dammit, Will," he grumbles, "can't you let an honest man sleep?" But the playwright, his eyes shining and the words tumbling out of his mouth, says, "Shut up and listen—tell me what you think of *this*!"

He begins to read to the still half-asleep Burbage, pacing around the room as he speaks. ". . . Whether 'tis nobler in the mind to suffer the slings and arrows of outrageous fortune—"

Burbage interrupts, suddenly wide awake, "That's excellent, very good, 'the slings and arrows of outrageous fortune,' yes, I think it will work quite well. . . ." He takes the parchment from Shakespeare and murmurs the lines to himself, slowly at first but with growing excitement.

The sun is just coming up, and the words of one of Shakespeare's most famous soliloquies are being uttered for the first time by the first actor ever to bring Hamlet to life. It must have been an exhilarating moment.

Shakespeare wrote most of his plays to be performed live by the actor Richard Burbage and the rest of the Lord Chamberlain's men (later the King's men). Today, however, our first encounter with the plays is usually in the form of the printed word. And there is no question that reading Shakespeare for the first time isn't easy. His plays aren't comic books or magazines or the dime-store detective novels I read when I was young. A lot of his sentences are complex. Many of his words are no longer used in our everyday speech. His profound thoughts are often condensed into poetry, which is not as straightforward as prose.

Yet when you hear the words spoken aloud, a lot of the language may strike you as unexpectedly modern. For Shakespeare's plays, like any dramatic work, weren't really meant to be read; they were meant to be spoken, seen, and performed. It's amazing how lines that are so troublesome in print can flow so naturally and easily when spoken.

I think it was precisely this music that first fascinated me. When I was growing up, Shakespeare was a stranger to me. I had no particular interest in him, for I was from a different cultural tradition. It never occurred to me that his plays might be more than just something to "get through" in school, like science or math or the physical education requirement we had to fulfill. My passions then were movies, radio, and vaudeville—certainly not Elizabethan drama.

I was, however, fascinated by words and language. Because I grew up in a home where Yiddish was spoken, and English was only a second language, I was acutely sensitive to the musical sounds of different languages and had an ear for lilt and cadence and rhythm in the spoken word. And so I loved reciting poems and speeches even as a very young child. In first grade I learned lots of short nature verses— "Who has seen the wind?," one of them began. My first foray into drama was playing the role of Scrooge in Charles Dickens's *A Christmas Carol* when I was eight years old. I liked summoning all the scorn and coldness I possessed and putting them into the words, "Bah, humbug!"

From there I moved on to longer and more famous poems and other works by writers of the 1930s. Then, in junior high school, I made my first acquaintance with Shakespeare through his play *Julius Caesar*. Our teacher, Miss McKay, assigned the class a passage to memorize from the opening scene of the play, the one that begins "Wherefore rejoice? What conquest brings he home?" The passage seemed so wonderfully theatrical and alive to me, and the experience of memorizing and reciting it was so much fun, that I went on to memorize another speech from the play on my own.

I chose Mark Antony's address to the crowd in Act 3,

scene 2, which struck me then as incredibly high drama.
Even today, when I speak the words, I feel the same thrill I
did that first time. There is the strong and athletic Antony
descending from the raised pulpit where he has been speaking, right into the midst of a crowded Roman square. Holding the torn and bloody cloak of the murdered Julius
Caesar in his hand, he begins to speak to the people of
Rome:

> If you have tears, prepare to shed them now.
> You all do know this mantle. I remember
> The first time ever Caesar put it on;
> 'Twas on a summer's evening in his tent,
> That day he overcame the Nervii.
> Look, in this place ran Cassius' dagger through.
> See what a rent the envious Casca made.
> Through this the well-belovèd Brutus stabbed,
> And as he plucked his cursèd steel away,
> Mark how the blood of Caesar followed it,
> As rushing out of doors to be resolved
> If Brutus so unkindly knocked or no;
> For Brutus, as you know, was Caesar's angel.
> Judge, O you gods, how dearly Caesar loved him!
> This was the most unkindest cut of all . . .

I'm not sure now that I even knew Shakespeare had written a lot of other plays, or that he was considered "timeless," "universal," or "classic"—but I knew a good speech
when I heard one, and I found the splendid rhythms of
Antony's rhetoric as exciting as anything I'd ever come
across.

Fifty years later, I still feel that way. Hearing good actors
speak Shakespeare gracefully and naturally is a wonderful
experience, unlike any other I know. There's a satisfying
fullness to the spoken word that the printed page just can't
convey. This is why seeing the plays of Shakespeare performed live in a theater is the best way to appreciate them.
If you can't do that, listening to sound recordings or watch-
ing film versions of the plays is the next best thing.

But if you do start with the printed word, use the play as a
script. Be an actor yourself and say the lines out loud. Don't
worry too much at first about words you don't immediately
understand. Look them up in the footnotes or a dictionary,

but don't spend too much time on this. It is more profitable (and fun) to get the sense of a passage and sing it out. Speak naturally, almost as if you were talking to a friend, but be sure to enunciate the words properly. You'll be surprised at how much you understand simply by speaking the speech "trippingly on the tongue," as Hamlet advises the Players.

You might start, as I once did, with a speech from *Julius Caesar*, in which the tribune (city official) Marullus scolds the commoners for transferring their loyalties so quickly from the defeated and murdered general Pompey to the newly victorious Julius Caesar:

> Wherefore rejoice? What conquest brings he home?
> What tributaries follow him to Rome
> To grace in captive bonds his chariot wheels?
> You blocks, you stones, you worse than senseless
>   things!
> O you hard hearts, you cruel men of Rome,
> Knew you not Pompey? Many a time and oft
> Have you climbed up to walls and battlements,
> To towers and windows, yea, to chimney tops,
> Your infants in your arms, and there have sat
> The livelong day, with patient expectation,
> To see great Pompey pass the streets of Rome.

With the exception of one or two words like "wherefore" (which means "why," not "where"), "tributaries" (which means "captives"), and "patient expectation" (which means patient waiting), the meaning and emotions of this speech can be easily understood.

From here you can go on to dialogues or other more challenging scenes. Although you may stumble over unaccustomed phrases or unfamiliar words at first, and even fall flat when you're crossing some particularly rocky passages, pick yourself up and stay with it. Remember that it takes time to feel at home with anything new. Soon you'll come to recognize Shakespeare's unique sense of humor and way of saying things as easily as you recognize a friend's laughter.

And then it will just be a matter of choosing which one of Shakespeare's plays you want to tackle next. As a true fan of his, you'll find that you're constantly learning from his plays. It's a journey of discovery that you can continue for the rest of your life. For no matter how many times you read or see a particular play, there will always be something new there that you won't have noticed before.

Why do so many thousands of people get hooked on Shakespeare and develop a habit that lasts a lifetime? What can he really say to us today, in a world filled with inventions and problems he never could have imagined? And how do you get past his special language and difficult sentence structure to understand him?

The best way to answer these questions is to go see a live production. You might not know much about Shakespeare, or much about the theater, but when you watch actors performing one of his plays on the stage, it will soon become clear to you why people get so excited about a playwright who lived hundreds of years ago.

For the story—what's happening in the play—is the most accessible part of Shakespeare. In *A Midsummer Night's Dream,* for example, you can immediately understand the situation: a girl is chasing a guy who's chasing a girl who's chasing another guy. No wonder *A Midsummer Night's Dream* is one of the most popular of Shakespeare's plays: it's about one of the world's most popular pastimes— falling in love.

But the course of true love never did run smooth, as the young suitor Lysander says. Often in Shakespeare's comedies the girl whom the guy loves doesn't love him back, or she loves him but he loves someone else. In *The Two Gentlemen of Verona*, Julia loves Proteus, Proteus loves Sylvia, and Sylvia loves Valentine, who is Proteus's best friend. In the end, of course, true love prevails, but not without lots of complications along the way.

For in all of his plays—comedies, histories, and tragedies—Shakespeare is showing you human nature. His characters act and react in the most extraordinary ways—and sometimes in the most incomprehensible ways. People are always trying to find motivations for what a character does. They ask, "Why does Iago want to destroy Othello?"

The answer, to me, is very simple—because that's the way Iago is. That's just his nature. Shakespeare doesn't explain his characters; he sets them in motion—and away they go. He doesn't worry about whether they're likable or not. He's interested in interesting people, and his most fascinating characters are those who are unpredictable. If you lean back in your chair early on in one of his plays, thinking you've figured out what Iago or Shylock (in *The Merchant of Venice*) is up to, don't be too sure—because that great judge of human nature, Shakespeare, will surprise you every time.

He is just as wily in the way he structures a play. In *Macbeth*, a comic scene is suddenly introduced just after the bloodiest and most treacherous slaughter imaginable, of a guest and king by his host and subject, when in comes a drunk porter who has to go to the bathroom. Shakespeare is tickling your emotions by bringing a stand-up comic on-stage right on the heels of a savage murder.

It has taken me thirty years to understand even some of these things, and so I'm not suggesting that Shakespeare is immediately understandable. I've gotten to know him not through theory but through practice, the practice of the *living* Shakespeare—the playwright of the theater.

Of course the plays are a great achievement of dramatic literature, and they should be studied and analyzed in schools and universities. But you must always remember, when reading all the words *about* the playwright and his plays, that *Shakespeare's* words came first and that in the end there is nothing greater than a single actor on the stage speaking the lines of Shakespeare.

Everything important that I know about Shakespeare comes from the practical business of producing and directing his plays in the theater. The task of classifying, criticizing, and editing Shakespeare's printed works I happily leave to others. For me, his plays really do live on the stage, not on the page. That is what he wrote them for and that is how they are best appreciated.

Although Shakespeare lived and wrote hundreds of years ago, his name rolls off my tongue as if he were my brother. As a producer and director, I feel that there is a professional relationship between us that spans the centuries. As a human being, I feel that Shakespeare has enriched my understanding of life immeasurably. I hope you'll let him do the same for you.

♣

I've always loved the scene in *Twelfth Night* where the steward Malvolio discovers the love letter addressed to him that he imagines was written by the Lady Olivia. In having Malvolio read it out loud, Shakespeare gives us a glimpse of a man whose fantastic ambitions and exaggerated sense of his own worth make him an obvious target for those in the play—Sir Toby Belch, Sir Andrew Aguecheek, Maria, and Fabian—who cannot tolerate his pomposity.

There's no question that Malvolio is the character of greatest interest to Shakespeare, because he subjects him to the cruellest kind of treatment at the hands of Olivia's alcoholic uncle and his cohorts. While the audience is led to enjoy the antics and mischief perpetrated on this puritanical figure, Shakespeare (as usual), is not content with a simplistic attitude toward this important character. Instead, the playwright encourages us to feel sympathetic toward Malvolio for his tribulations in the later scene, tribulations that seem overly severe.

At the end of the play, Feste, the Fool, echoes the very words that Malvolio himself uttered in reading the planted letter: "Some are born great, some achieve greatness, and some have greatness thrust upon them." These words linger in our minds as we apply them to the world outside the play. We think of people who *are* born great and seem to have a natural genius; others who achieve greatness through hard work in the arts, in the sciences, in sports, in politics; and still others who unexpectedly have greatness thrust upon them, such as a vice president who may suddenly become the president of the United States after an assassination or a resignation.

JOSEPH PAPP

JOSEPH PAPP GRATEFULLY ACKNOWLEDGES THE HELP OF
ELIZABETH KIRKLAND IN PREPARING THIS FOREWORD.

Introduction

Twelfth Night is possibly the latest of the three festive comedies, including *Much Ado about Nothing* and *As You Like It*, with which Shakespeare climaxed his distinctively philosophical and joyous vein of comic writing. Performed on February 2, 1602, at the Middle Temple (one of the Inns of Court, where young men studied law) and written possibly as early as 1599, *Twelfth Night* is usually dated 1600 or 1601. This play is indeed the most festive of the lot. Its keynote is Saturnalian release and the carnival pursuit of love and mirth. Along with such familiar motifs (found, for example, in *As You Like It* and *The Merchant of Venice*) as the plucky heroine disguised as a man, *Twelfth Night* also returns to the more farcical routines of mistaken identity found in Shakespeare's early comedy. As a witness of the 1602 performance, John Manningham, observed, the play is "much like the *Comedy of Errors*, or *Menaechmi* in Plautus, but most like and near to that in Italian called *Inganni*." Manningham might have added Shakespeare's *The Two Gentlemen of Verona* as another early instance, since it too employs the device of the heroine, Julia, disguised in the service of her unresponsive lover, Proteus.

The carnival atmosphere is appropriate to the season designated in the play's title: the twelfth night of Christmas, January 6, the Feast of Epiphany. (The prologue to *Gl'Ingannati*, perhaps the Italian play referred to by Manningham, speaks of "La Notte di Beffania," Epiphany night.) Although Epiphany has of course a primary Christian significance as the Feast of the Magi, it was also in Renaissance times the last day of the Christmas revels. Over a twelve-day period, from Christmas until January 6, noble households sponsored numerous performances of plays, masques, banquets, and every kind of festivity. (Leslie Hotson argues, in fact, that *Twelfth Night* was first performed on twelfth night in early 1601, in the presence of Queen Elizabeth.) Students left schools for vacations, celebrating release from study with plays and revels of their own. The stern rigors of a rule-bound society gave way temporarily to playful inversions of authority. The reign of the Boy Bishop and the Feast of Fools, for example, gave choristers and minor church functionaries the cherished opportunity to boss the hierarchy around, mock the liturgy with outrageous lampooning, and generally let off steam. Although such customs occasionally got out of hand, the idea was to channel potentially destructive insubordination into playacting and thereby promote harmony. Behind these Elizabethan midwinter customs lies the Roman Saturnalia, with its pagan spirit of gift-giving, sensual indulgence, and satirical hostility to those who would curb merriment.

Shakespeare's choice of sources for *Twelfth Night* underscores his commitment to mirth. Renaissance literature offered numerous instances of mistaken identity among twins and of the disguised heroine serving as page to her beloved. Among those in English were the anonymous play *Sir Clyomon and Sir Clamydes* (c. 1570–1583), Sidney's *Arcadia* (1590), and the prose romance *Parismus* by Emmanuel Forde (1598), featuring both a shipwreck and two characters with the names of Olivia and Violetta. Of particular significance, but largely for negative reasons, is Barnabe Riche's tale of "Apollonius and Silla" in *Riche His Farewell to Military Profession* (1581), which was based on François de Belleforest's 1571 French version of Matteo Bandello's *Novelle* (1554). Here we find most of the requisite plot elements: the shipwreck; Silla's disguise as a page in Duke Apollonius's court; her office as ambassador of love from Apollonius to the Lady Julina, who thereupon falls in love with Silla; the arrival of Silla's twin brother, Silvio; and his consequent success in winning Julina's affection. To Riche, however, this tale is merely a long warning against the enervating power of infatuation. Silvio gets Julina with child and disappears forthwith, making his belated reappearance almost too late to save the wrongly accused Silla. Riche's moralizing puts the blame on the gross and drunken appetite of carnal love. The total mismatching of affection with which the story begins, and the sudden realignments of desire based on mere outward resemblances, are seen as proofs of love's unreasonableness. Shakespeare of course retains and capitalizes on the irrational quality of love, as in *A Midsummer Night's Dream*, but in doing so he minimizes the harm done (Olivia is not made pregnant) and repudiates any negative moral judgments. The added subplot, with its rebuking of Malvolio's censoriousness, may have been conceived as a further answer to Riche, Fenton, and their sober school.

Shakespeare's festive spirit owes much, as Manningham observed, to Plautus and the neoclassical Italian comic writers. At least three Italian comedies called *Gl'Inganni* ("The Frauds") employ the motif of mistaken identity, and one of them, by Curzio Gonzaga (1592), supplies Viola's assumed name of "Cesare," or Cesario. Another play with the same title appeared in 1562. More useful is *Gl'Ingannati* ("The Deceived"), performed in 1531, translated into French in 1543. Besides a plot line generally similar to that of *Twelfth Night*, and the reference to "La Notte di Beffania" (Epiphany), this play offers the suggestive name *Malevolti*, "evil-faced," and *Fabio* (which resembles "Fabian"). It also contains possible hints for Malvolio, Toby, and company, although the plot of the counterfeit letter is original with Shakespeare. Essentially, Shakespeare superimposes his own subplot on an Italianate novella plot, as he did in *The Taming of the Shrew* and *Much Ado about Nothing*. And it is in the Malvolio story that Shakespeare most pointedly defends merriment. Feste, the professional fool, an original stage type for Shakespeare in *Twelfth Night* and in *As You Like It*, also reinforces the theme of seizing the moment of mirth.

This great lesson, of savoring life's pleasures while one is still young, is something that Orsino and Olivia have not yet learned when the play commences. Although suited to each other in rank, wealth, and attractiveness, they are unable to overcome their own willful posturing in the elaborate charade of courtship. Like Silvius in *As You Like It*, Orsino is the conventional wooer trapped in the courtly artifice of love's rules. He opens the play on a cloying note of self-pity. He is fascinated with his own degradation as a rejected suitor, and bores his listeners with his changeable moods and fondness for poetical "conceits." He sees himself as a hart pursued by his desires "like fell and cruel hounds," reminding us that enervating lovesickness has in fact robbed him of his manly occupation, hunting. He sends ornately contrived messages to Olivia but has not seen her in so long that his passion has become unreal and fantastical, feeding on itself.

Olivia plays the opposite role of chaste, denying woman-hood. She explains her retirement from the world as mourning for a dead brother (whose name we never learn) but this withdrawal from life is another unreal vision. Olivia's practice of mourning, whereby she will "water once a day her chamber round / With eye-offending brine" (1.1.28–29), is a lifeless ritual. As others view the matter, she is senselessly wasting her beauty and affection on the dead. "What a plague means my niece to take the death of her brother thus?" Sir Toby expostulates (1.3.1–2). Viola, though she too has seemingly lost a brother, is an important foil in this regard, for she continues to hope for her broth-er's safety, trusts his soul is in heaven if he is dead, and refuses to give up her commitment to life in any case. We suspect that Olivia takes a willful pleasure in self-denial not unlike Orsino's self-congratulatory suffering. She ap-pears to derive satisfaction from the power she holds over Orsino, a power of refusal. And she must know that she looks stunning in black.

Olivia's household reflects in part her mood of self-denial. She keeps Malvolio as steward because he too dresses somberly, insists on quiet as befits a house in mourning, and maintains order. Yet Olivia also retains a fool, Feste, who is Malvolio's opposite in every way. Hard-pressed to defend his mirthful function in a household so given over to melancholy, Feste must find some way of per-suading his mistress that her very gravity is itself the es-sence of folly. This is a paradox, because sobriety and order appeal to the conventional wisdom of the world. Malvolio, sensing that his devotion to propriety is being challenged by the fool's prating, chides Olivia for taking "delight in such a barren rascal" (1.5.80–81).

Feste must argue for an inversion of appearance and real-ity whereby many of the world's ordinary pursuits can be seen to be ridiculous. As he observes, in his habitually ellip-tical manner of speech, "*cucullus non facit monachum* [the cowl doesn't make the monk]; that's as much to say as I wear not motley in my brain" (1.5.52–54). Feste wins his case by making Olivia laugh at her own illogic in grieving for a brother whose soul she assumes to be in heaven. By extension, Olivia has indeed been a fool for allowing herself to be deprived of happiness in love by her brother's death ("there is no true cuckold but calamity"), and for failing to consider the brevity of youth ("beauty's a flower"). Yet, paradoxically, only one who professes to be a fool can point this out, enabled by his detachment and innocence to perceive simple but profound truths denied to supposedly rational persons. This vision of the fool as naturally wise, and of society as self-indulgently insane, fascinated Renaissance writers, from Erasmus in *In Praise of Folly* and Cervantes in *Don Quixote* to Shakespeare in *King Lear*.

Viola, although not dressed in motley, aligns herself with Feste's rejection of self-denial. Refreshingly, even comically, she challenges the staid artifice of Orsino's and Olivia's lives. She is an ocean traveler, like many of Shakespeare's later heroines (Marina in *Pericles*, Perdita in *The Winter's Tale*), arriving on Illyria's shore plucky and determined. On her first embassy to Olivia from Orsino, she exposes with disarming candor the willfully ritualistic quality of Olivia's existence. Viola discards the flowery set speech she had prepared and memorized at Orsino's behest; despite her charmingly conceited assertion that the speech has been "excellently well penned," she senses that its elegant but empty rhetoric is all too familiar to the disdainful Olivia. Instead, Viola departs from her text to urge seizing the moment of happiness. "You do usurp yourself," she lectures Olivia, "for what is yours to bestow is not yours to reserve" (1.5.183–184). Beauty is a gift of nature, and failure to use it is a sin against nature. Or, again, "Lady, you are the cruel'st she alive / If you will lead these graces [Olivia's beauty] to the grave / And leave the world no copy" (236–238). An essential argument in favor of love, as in Shakespeare's sonnets, is the necessity of marriage and childbearing in order to perpetuate beauty. This approach is new to Olivia, and catches her wholly by surprise. In part she reacts, like Phoebe in *As You Like It*, with perverse logic, rejecting a too-willing wooer for one who is hard to get. Yet Olivia is also attracted by a new note of sincerity, prompting her to reenter life and accept maturely both the risks and rewards of romantic involvement. Her longing for Cesario is of course sexually misdirected, but the appearance of Viola's identical twin, Sebastian, soon puts all to rights.

The motifs of Olivia's attraction for another woman (both

actors would have been boys), and of Orsino's deep fondness for Cesario that matures into sexual love, delicately evoke homosexual suggestions as in *As You Like It*. Once again, however, we must approach the notion circumspectly, remembering that these elements are also found in Shakespeare's sources and reflect a convention wholly different from a modern psychological analysis of sexual aberration. Like Rosalind, Viola uses her male attire to win Orsino's pure affection, in a friendship devoid of sexual interest since both seemingly are men. Viola as Cesario can teach Orsino about the conventions of love in relaxed and frank conversations that would not be possible if she were known to be a woman. She teaches him to avoid the beguiling but misleading myths of Petrarchan love (named after the Italian sonneteer Francis Petrarch, whose poems embody the idealization of courtly love), and so prepares him for the realities of marriage. Comparing men and women in love, she confides, "We men may say more, swear more, but indeed / Our shows are more than will; for still we prove / Much in our vows, but little in our love" (2.4.116–118). Once she and Orsino have achieved an instinctive rapport all the more remarkable for their talking so often at cross-purposes, Viola's unmasking can make possible a physical communion as well. The friendship of Sebastian and Antonio, sorely tested by the mix-ups of the mistaken identity plot, presents further insight into the debate of love and friendship.

The belowstairs characters of the subplot, Sir Toby and the rest, share with Feste and Viola a commitment to joy. As Sir Toby proclaims in his first speech, "care's an enemy to life" (1.3.2–3). Even the simpleton Sir Andrew, although gulled by Sir Toby into spending his money on a hopeless pursuit of Olivia, seems none the worse for his treatment; he loves to drink in Sir Toby's company and can afford to pay for his entertainment. Sir Toby gives us some of the richly inventive humor of Falstaff, another lovable fat roguish knight. In this subplot, however, the confrontations between merriment and sobriety are more harshly drawn than in the main plot. Whereas the gracious Olivia is won away from her folly, the obdurate Malvolio can only be exposed to ridicule. He is chiefly to blame for the polarization of attitudes, for he insists on rebuking the mirth of others. His name (*Mal-volio*, the "ill-wisher") implies a self-satisfied determination to impose his rigid moral code on others. As Sir Toby taunts him, "Dost thou think, because thou art virtuous, there shall be no more cakes and ale?" (2.3.114–115). Malvolio's inflexible hostility provokes a desire for comic vengeance. The method is satiric: the clever manipulators, Maria and Toby, invent a scheme to entrap Malvolio in his own self-deceit. The punishment fits the crime, for he has long dreamed of himself as Count Malvolio, rich, powerful, in a position to demolish Toby and the rest. Without Malvolio's infatuated predisposition to believe that Olivia could actually love him and write such a letter as he finds, Maria's scheme would have no hope of success. He tortures the text to make it yield a suitable meaning, much in the style of Puritan theologizing.

Indeed, Malvolio does in some ways resemble a Puritan, as Maria observes (2.3.139–147), even though she qualifies the assertion by saying that he is not a religious fanatic but a "time-pleaser." She directs her observation not at a religious group but at all who would be killjoys; if the Puritans are like that, she intimates, so much the worse for them. This uncharacteristic lack of charity gives a sharp tone to the vengeance practiced on Malvolio, evoking from Olivia a protestation that "He hath been most notoriously abused" (5.1.379). The belated attempt to make a reconciliation with him seems, however, doomed to failure, in light of his grim resolve to "be revenged on the whole pack of you." At the height of his discomfiture he has been tricked into doing the two things he hates most: smiling affably, and wearing sportive attire. The appearance of merriment is so grossly unsuited to him that he is declared mad and put into safe-keeping. The apostle of sobriety in this play thus comes before us as a declared madman, while the fool Feste offers him sage comment in the guise of a priest. Wisdom and folly have changed places. The upside-down character of the play is epitomized in Malvolio's plaintive remark to Feste (no longer posing as the priest): "I am as well in my wits, Fool, as thou art" (4.2.88). Malvolio's comeuppance is richly deserved, but the severity of vengeance and counter-vengeance suggests that the triumph of festival will not last long. This brevity is, of course, inherent in the nature of such holiday release from responsibility. As Feste sings, "What's to come is still unsure. / In delay there lies no plenty."

Twelfth Night
in Performance

Although *Twelfth Night* has almost always been popular onstage, many theatrical producers in past years have treated
the play as though its stage popularity had to be achieved in
defiance of the text rather than through it. Not until recently have they trusted the play to conjure up its own sense
of magic and imagination; too often they have relied, coun-
terproductively, on excessively detailed realism instead of
theatrical evocation. This literalized and revisionistic approach dominated much of the play's stage history during
the Restoration and the eighteenth and nineteenth centuries, despite evidence that *Twelfth Night* (presumably as
Shakespeare wrote it) was very popular in his own day and
for some time after. Following his death the play was staged
at court in 1618 and 1622, and, along with *Much Ado about
Nothing*, it was identified by the poet Leonard Digges in
1640 as still among Shakespeare's most popular dramas.
Digges suggested one important reason for this popularity
when he commented that crowds were filling the theater
"To hear *Malvolio*, that cross-gartered gull." Digges's observation also points to a distortion that would occur in
subsequent productions of *Twelfth Night:* the play would
become a vehicle for lead actors and actresses in a few key
roles at the expense of the play as a whole. Revision of this
sort was common in the Restoration and eighteenth century, whereas scenic overemphasis came to be a predictable
feature of much nineteenth-century production.

The diarist Samuel Pepys saw a version of *Twelfth Night*
on three occasions in the 1660s and thought it "a silly
play." What Pepys objected to can perhaps be surmised
from Charles Burnaby's adaptation in 1703, called *Love Be-
trayed, or the Agreeable Disappointment*, in which Burnaby
undertook to "improve" the play with the kind of symmetry
and neoclassical unity that he evidently felt it lacked. In
this version, produced at the theater in Lincoln's Inn
Fields, London, Malvolio, having been merged with the
character of Sir Andrew, is tricked into fighting an abortive

comic duel with the disguised Viola, whom he believes to be
his rival for the love of Olivia. Maria becomes two characters, one an old servant in love with Sir Toby and the other a
confidante of Olivia. Sebastian is provided with a wise-
cracking servant. The characters are all renamed, and only
some fifty-eight lines of Shakespeare's text (including "If
music be the food of love, play on") remain intact. The major effect of Burnaby's revision is to reduce the number of
subplots and to bring to the foreground the opposition of
Malvolio and Viola. Malvolio is no longer the focus of a separate comic plot but at the center of the play, where, audiences evidently felt, he belonged.

Something more like Shakespeare's original of *Twelfth
Night* did return in 1741, to the Theatre Royal, Drury Lane,
evidently at the actor Charles Macklin's instigation (and
with Macklin as Malvolio), and enjoyed during the next century a number of popular runs. John Henderson and John
Philip Kemble, among others, took the part of Malvolio,
while Hannah Pritchard, Peg Woffington, Dorothea Jordan
(paired with her brother, George Bland, as Sebastian),
Sarah Siddons, and Helen Faucit played Viola. Feste's concluding song, customarily absent throughout the eighteenth century, was finally restored in 1799. Nevertheless,
adaptation continued to be a major factor in eighteenth-
and nineteenth-century productions of the play. Songs were
frequently added. Frederic Reynolds produced an operatic
version in 1820 at the Theatre Royal, Covent Garden, with
an overture compiled from various composers including
Thomas Morley, Thomas Ravenscroft, and Mozart. "Full
many a glorious morning" was introduced from the sonnets, "Even as the sun" from *Venus and Adonis,* "Orpheus
with his lute" from *Henry VIII,* and "Come unto these yellow sands" from *The Tempest,* all set off by elegant scenery
in what was supposed to be the style of the architect and set
designer Inigo Jones.

Even when Shakespeare's text was treated with more respect, the emphasis on lead actors and actresses remained
an unavoidable feature of nineteenth-century production.
At the Haymarket Theatre in London in 1846, Charlotte and
Susan Cushman, famous for their epicene Romeo and Juliet, starred as Viola and Olivia and made their pairing the
center of the theatrical experience. When Samuel Phelps

produced the play at the Sadler's Wells Theatre in 1848 and
again in 1857, he gave prominence to his own portrayal of
Malvolio as a grave and self-important Spanish grandee. In
1849, at the Theatre Royal, Marrylebone, Cora Mowatt and
Fanny Vining (who, like the Cushmans, had done an epicene
Romeo and Juliet) emulated their predecessors by pairing
themselves in the roles of Olivia and Viola.

Twelfth Night does not call for the spectacular effects of
battle sieges and royal pageantry that gave such impressive
scope to the epic productions of the history plays by
Charles Kean and others (as, for example, in Kean's *King
John*), but theater managers who were insistent on visual
opulence soon found a way to dress *Twelfth Night* in the
splendor they wished to emphasize. Kean opened at the
Princess's Theatre in 1850 with *Twelfth Night* and performed it some forty times, bestowing upon the play every
realistic scenic device known to nineteenth-century theater.
Henry Irving chose for his 1884 production, at the Lyceum
Theatre, London, a Venetian setting in the age of Queen
Elizabeth. Orsino's palace and Olivia's scarcely less pala-
tial villa were sumptuously Palladian in decor, while the art
of landscape gardening, as a contemporary observer mar-
veled, appeared "to have reached a very high pitch of excellence." Olivia's house featured an adjoining cloister. No
less impressive were the depictions of the seacoast, the
courtyard and terrace of Olivia's house, the road near
Olivia's house, and the dungeon for Malvolio. Ellen Terry
played a spritely Viola opposite Irving's sentimental Malvolio, and although the performance was not a success, it was
not for lack of handsome scene design.

In 1894, not to be outdone, producer Augustin Daly, at his
Daly's Theatre in London, began with an exciting storm
scene worthy of *The Tempest*. Unexpectedly, Daly showed
his audiences the landing of Sebastian and Antonio rather
than that of Viola and the Captain, which allowed the production's star, Ada Rehan (Viola), to enter more impres-
sively in the next scene. The rearrangement also made
possible the employment of an elaborate set for the Duke's
palace. So elaborate was this set that, in order to keep it in
use for a continuous stretch of dramatic action, Daly ran
together Act 1, scene 1 (showing Orsino's love melancholy),
with Act 1, scene 4 (in which Viola as Cesario is dispatched

to Olivia), before making the cumbersome shift to Olivia's
house. Once there, Daly devised another long composite
scene, in which Toby and Andrew carouse (1.3), Olivia receives Viola-Cesario (1.5), and Malvolio returns the ring to
Viola-Cesario (2.2). Music was prominent throughout the
production. During its first scene, for instance, on the seacoast after the storm happy villagers sang "Come unto
these yellow sands" from *The Tempest;* other songs were introduced into the scenes at Olivia's house. Moonlight
beamed onto the set as Orsino's minstrels sang "Who is
Olivia?" (taken from "Who is Sylvia?" in *The Two Gentlemen of Verona*) set to music by Franz Schubert. Rehan, the
scenery, and the music made the play a great success; it ran
for 119 performances.

Herbert Beerbohm Tree's *Twelfth Night,* at Her Majesty's
Theatre in 1901, achieved a kind of pinnacle in the verisimilar staging of *Twelfth Night.* His set for Olivia's house featured a terrace that extended to the extreme back of the
stage and a garden complete with real grass, fountains,
pathways, and descending steps. It was, according to an
eyewitness report, literally an Italian garden, going beyond
anything hitherto seen in beauty and realistic illusion. As in
Daly's production, the set was so nearly immovable that
scenes had to be rearranged extensively, even to the point of
staging in Olivia's garden some dramatic material that
properly belonged at Orsino's court or elsewhere. Tree also
focused, in traditional nineteenth-century fashion, on the
leading characters, playing Malvolio himself to the Viola of
Lily Brayton.

Nonetheless, a major new direction was at hand. Already,
in 1895, *Twelfth Night* had become the first of the revivals
by actor-manager William Poel and the Elizabethan Stage
Society, who staged it once at Burlington Hall, Savile Row,
and again at St. George's Hall. Featuring Elizabethan costumes, a stage bare of scenery, and a single ten-minute
intermission, the production tried to approximate the
conditions of Shakespeare's own theater. Two years later, in
a production in the Hall of the Middle Temple (one of the
Inns of Court, where young men studied law in London),
Poel sought to produce the play as it might have been done
at Shakespeare's Blackfriars Theatre. A table and chair
were the only props on the raised platform stage, which was

surrounded by halberdiers (guards); costumes were based on the dress of the Elizabethan court, and the songs were, wherever possible, given their original settings and played on sixteenth-century instruments.

In the spirit of Poel's reforms, the twentieth century has generally turned against the excesses of nineteenth-century verisimilar staging. The anti-illusionism implicit in Poel's attempts to restore Elizabethan staging practices was successfully translated into a more modern idiom in a swift-moving ensemble production directed by Harley Granville-Barker at London's Savoy Theatre in 1912, and then in a performance on an apron stage (i.e., a stage thrust out in front of the proscenium) directed by Barry Jackson at the Birmingham Repertory Theatre in 1913, which was revived in 1916 with an uncut text. Since then the play has had its share of new settings and adaptations, including a rock musical version called *Your Own Thing* (1968), but on the whole, of all Shakespeare's comedies *Twelfth Night* seems the least in need of being made "relevant." Allowed to speak for itself, the play has had memorable theatrical triumphs. Tyrone Guthrie's London production at the Old Vic in 1937 successfully doubled Jessica Tandy as Viola and Sebastian and had Laurence Olivier as Toby and Alec Guinness as Andrew Aguecheek. In 1954 the play again graced the Old Vic, directed by Denis Carey, with Claire Bloom as an energetic, almost ferocious Viola and Richard Burton as Toby. A year later, John Gielgud directed Vivien Leigh as Viola and Olivier as Malvolio at Stratford-upon-Avon. John Barton's 1969 Stratford-upon-Avon production was movingly autumnal, dominated by Emrys James's melancholy Feste.

Elizabethan costuming, which was used in Barton's production, seems admirably suited to the play's winsome blend of satire and foolery about love; onstage the play seems quintessentially of Shakespeare's age and yet timeless. It can fully employ the talents of repertory companies expert in ensemble work and willing to distribute the acting honors beyond the roles of Viola, Toby, and Feste. It is a favorite of amateurs, and acts well out-of-doors. It has become a staple of summer festivals at Stratford, in Canada, at Ashland, in Oregon, and many others, where a sturdy and rollicking performance can be counted on to pack the house. New interpretation is usually a matter not of a wholly new or of an anachronistic setting but of nuance, as in the 1969 Barton production when Malvolio, played by Donald Sinden, coming onstage in Act 3, scene 4, stopped to correct the sundial by consulting his pocket watch; the gratuitous officiousness of the gesture was comically eloquent.

Apron, or thrust, stages and quick-paced productions of recent years enable actors to stage *Twelfth Night* much as it must have been performed in Shakespeare's Globe Theatre. The scene of eavesdropping on Malvolio (2.5), for instance, requires only that the actors playing Sir Toby and his belowstairs companions hide themselves where their antics can be visible to spectators during the reading of the letter; on Shakespeare's stage, the pillars would have been especially convenient for such a purpose. When they performed the play at Middle Temple Hall, in February of 1602, as John Manningham's diary tells us, the actors would have had the magnificent screen with its two arched doorways and other architectural features in which to hide from Malvolio or, later, for use as a makeshift prison in which to incarcerate him. The comic duel of Sir Andrew and Viola-Cesario requires only that the contenders approach one another from opposite entrances, with Sir Toby and Fabian moving back and forth between the two unwilling contenders to frighten them or propose terms.

When, in Act 2, scene 2, Malvolio hastens after Viola-Cesario and encounters him in a street, no stage business is required other than that they enter *at several* (i.e., separate) *doors*. They need not (and indeed are instructed that they should not) enter one after the other by the same door to signify that they are coming from Olivia's house, for doors are not used in this illusionistic way on the Shakespearean stage. The previous scene, in any case, has been located in an entirely different part of Illyria, so that Shakespeare makes no attempt to provide a visual continuity between the end of Act 1, scene 5, when Cesario-Viola leaves Olivia's house with Malvolio in pursuit, and their meeting in Act 2, scene 2. Instead, Elizabethan theatrical convention asks the audience to understand that actors entering by separate doors are encountering one another. Realistically identified doorways, or, in the scene of eavesdropping, real shrubbery, not only slow down changes of scene but miss the point by literalizing Illyria. The world in which *Twelfth Night* is located is, or should be, one of theatrical imagination. Illyria is above all a place of the artist's creation, his play world, his theater. *Twelfth Night* frequently calls attention to its self-reflexive quality, as when Fabian says of Malvolio's comic discomfiture, "If this were played upon a stage now, I could condemn it as an improbable fiction" (3.4.129–130). Shakespeare's play revels in this paradox of illusion, making improbable fiction wholly convincing and defying the more ordinary conventions by which dramatic art is made to appear "real."

The Playhouse

This early copy of a drawing by Johannes de Witt of the Swan Theatre in London (c. 1596), made by his friend Arend van Buchell, is the only surviving contemporary sketch of the interior of a public theater in the 1590s.

From other contemporary evidence, including the stage directions and dialogue of Elizabethan plays, we can surmise that the various public theaters where Shakespeare's plays were produced (the Theatre, the Curtain, the Globe) resembled the Swan in many important particulars, though there must have been some variations as well. The public playhouses were essentially round, or polygonal, and open to the sky, forming an acting arena approximately 70 feet in diameter; they did not have a large curtain with which to open and close a scene, such as we see today in opera and some traditional theater. A platform measuring approximately 43 feet across and 27 feet deep, referred to in the de Witt drawing as the *proscaenium*, projected into the yard, *planities sive arena*. The roof, *tectum*, above the stage and supported by two pillars, could contain machinery for ascents and descents, as were required in several of Shakespeare's late plays. Above this roof was a hut, shown in the drawing with a flag flying atop it and a trumpeter at its door announcing the performance of a play. The underside of the stage roof, called the heavens, was usually richly decorated with symbolic figures of the sun, the moon, and the constellations. The platform stage stood at a height of 5½ feet or so above the yard, providing room under the stage for underworldly effects. A trapdoor, which is not visible in this drawing, gave access to the space below.

The structure at the back of the platform (labeled *mimorum aedes*), known as the tiring-house because it was the actors' attiring (dressing) space, featured at least two doors, as shown here. Some theaters seem to have also had a discovery space, or curtained recessed alcove, perhaps between the two doors—in which Falstaff could have hidden from the sheriff (*1 Henry IV*, 2.4) or Polonius could have eavesdropped on Hamlet and his mother (*Hamlet*, 3.4). This discovery space probably gave the actors a means of access to and from the tiring-house. Curtains may also have been hung in front of the stage doors on occasion. The de Witt drawing shows a gallery above the doors that extends across the back and evidently contains spectators. On occasions when action "above" demanded the use of this space, as when Juliet appears at her "window" (*Romeo and Juliet*, 2.2 and 3.5), the gallery seems to have been used by the actors, but large scenes there were impractical.

The three-tiered auditorium is perhaps best described by Thomas Platter, a visitor to London in 1599 who saw on that occasion Shakespeare's *Julius Caesar* performed at the Globe:

> The playhouses are so constructed that they play on a raised platform, so that everyone has a good view. There are different galleries and places [*orchestra, sedilia, porticus*], however, where the seating is better and more comfortable and therefore more expensive. For whoever cares to stand below only pays one English penny, but if he wishes to sit, he enters by another door [*ingressus*] and pays another penny, while if he desires to sit in the most comfortable seats, which are cushioned, where he not only sees everything well but can also be seen, then he pays yet another English penny at another door. And during the performance food and drink are carried round the audience, so that for what one cares to pay one may also have refreshment.

Scenery was not used, though the theater building itself was handsome enough to invoke a feeling of order and hierarchy that lent itself to the splendor and pageantry onstage. Portable properties, such as thrones, stools, tables, and beds, could be carried or thrust on as needed. In the scene pictured here by de Witt, a lady on a bench, attended perhaps by her waiting-gentlewoman, receives the address of a male figure. If Shakespeare had written *Twelfth Night* by 1596 for performance at the Swan, we could imagine Malvolio appearing like this as he bows before the Countess Olivia and her gentlewoman, Maria.

TWELFTH NIGHT
or
WHAT YOU WILL

[*Dramatis Personae*

ORSINO, *Duke (or Count) of Illyria*
VALENTINE, *gentleman attending on Orsino*
CURIO, *gentleman attending on Orsino*

VIOLA, *a shipwrecked lady, later disguised as Cesario*
SEBASTIAN, *twin brother of Viola*
ANTONIO, *a sea captain, friend to Sebastian*
CAPTAIN *of the shipwrecked vessel*

OLIVIA, *a rich countess of Illyria*
MARIA, *gentlewoman in Olivia's household*
SIR TOBY BELCH, *Olivia's uncle*
SIR ANDREW AGUECHEEK, *a companion of Sir Toby*
MALVOLIO, *steward of Olivia's household*
FABIAN, *a member of Olivia's household*
FESTE, *a clown, also called* FOOL, *Olivia's jester*

A PRIEST
FIRST OFFICER
SECOND OFFICER

Lords, Sailors, Musicians, and other Attendants

SCENE: *A city in Illyria, and the seacoast near it*]

1.1   *Enter Orsino Duke of Illyria, Curio, and other lords [with musicians].*

ORSINO
  If music be the food of love, play on;
  Give me excess of it, that surfeiting,
  The appetite may sicken and so die.
  That strain again! It had a dying fall;   4
  O, it came o'er my ear like the sweet sound
  That breathes upon a bank of violets,
  Stealing and giving odor. Enough, no more.
  'Tis not so sweet now as it was before.
  O spirit of love, how quick and fresh art thou,   9
  That, notwithstanding thy capacity
  Receiveth as the sea, naught enters there,
  Of what validity and pitch soe'er,   12
  But falls into abatement and low price   13
  Even in a minute. So full of shapes is fancy   14
  That it alone is high fantastical.   15

CURIO
  Will you go hunt, my lord?

ORSINO   What, Curio?

CURIO   The hart.

ORSINO
  Why, so I do, the noblest that I have.   17
  O, when mine eyes did see Olivia first,
  Methought she purged the air of pestilence.
  That instant was I turned into a hart,
  And my desires, like fell and cruel hounds,   21
  E'er since pursue me.

      Enter Valentine.

                          How now, what news from her?   22

1.1. Location: Orsino's court.
s.d. Illyria country on the east coast of the Adriatic Sea   **4 fall** cadence   **9 quick and fresh** keen and hungry   **12 validity** value.   **pitch** superiority. (Literally, the highest point of a falcon's flight.)   **13 abatement** depreciation   **14 shapes** imagined forms.   **fancy** love   **15 it . . . fantastical** it surpasses everything else in imaginative power   **17 the noblest . . . have** i.e., my noblest part, my heart (punning on *hart*)
21 fell fierce   **22 pursue me** (Alludes to the story in Ovid of Actaeon, who, having seen Diana bathing, was transformed into a stag and killed by his own hounds.)

VALENTINE
　So please my lord, I might not be admitted,
　But from her handmaid do return this answer:
　The element itself, till seven years' heat,   25
　Shall not behold her face at ample view;
　But like a cloistress she will veilèd walk,   27
　And water once a day her chamber round
　With eye-offending brine—all this to season   29
　A brother's dead love, which she would keep fresh   30
　And lasting in her sad remembrance.

ORSINO
　O, she that hath a heart of that fine frame   32
　To pay this debt of love but to a brother,
　How will she love, when the rich golden shaft   34
　Hath killed the flock of all affections else   35
　That live in her; when liver, brain, and heart,   36
　These sovereign thrones, are all supplied, and filled   37
　Her sweet perfections, with one self king!   38
　Away before me to sweet beds of flowers.
　Love thoughts lie rich when canopied with bowers.

　　　　　　　　　　　　　　　　　　　　　　　　　Exeunt.

❖

1.2　　*Enter Viola, a Captain, and sailors.*

VIOLA　What country, friends, is this?
CAPTAIN　This is Illyria, lady.
VIOLA
　And what should I do in Illyria?
　My brother he is in Elysium.   4

25 element sky. **seven years' heat** seven summers **27 cloistress** nun
secluded in a religious community **29 season** keep fresh (playing on
the idea of the salt in her tears) **30 brother's dead** dead brother's
32 frame construction **34 golden shaft** i.e., of Cupid **35 affections else**
other feelings **36 liver, brain, and heart** (In medieval and Elizabethan
psychology these organs were the seats of the passions, of thought, and
of feeling.) **37 supplied** filled **37–38 and . . . perfections** and her sweet
perfections filled **38 self king** single lord (the object of her entire
affection)

1.2. Location: The seacoast.
4 Elysium classical abode of the blessed dead

Perchance he is not drowned. What think you, sailors? 5
CAPTAIN
It is perchance that you yourself were saved.   6
VIOLA
O, my poor brother! And so perchance may he be.
CAPTAIN
True, madam, and to comfort you with chance,   8
Assure yourself, after our ship did split,
When you and those poor number saved with you
Hung on our driving boat, I saw your brother,   11
Most provident in peril, bind himself,
Courage and hope both teaching him the practice,
To a strong mast that lived upon the sea;   14
Where, like Arion on the dolphin's back,   15
I saw him hold acquaintance with the waves
So long as I could see.
VIOLA   For saying so, there's gold. [*She gives money.*]
Mine own escape unfoldeth to my hope,   19
Whereto thy speech serves for authority,   20
The like of him. Know'st thou this country?   21
CAPTAIN
Ay, madam, well, for I was bred and born
Not three hours' travel from this very place.
VIOLA   Who governs here?
CAPTAIN
A noble duke, in nature as in name.
VIOLA   What is his name?
CAPTAIN   Orsino.
VIOLA
Orsino! I have heard my father name him.
He was a bachelor then.
CAPTAIN
And so is now, or was so very late;
For but a month ago I went from hence,

5–6 Perchance . . . perchance perhaps . . . by mere chance   **8 chance**
i.e., what one may hope that chance will bring about   **11 driving** drift-
ing, driven by the seas   **14 lived** i.e., kept afloat   **15 Arion** a Greek poet
who so charmed the dolphins with his lyre that they saved him when he
leaped into the sea to escape murderous sailors   **19–21 unfoldeth . . .
him** i.e., offers a hopeful example that he may have escaped similarly, to
which hope your speech provides support

And then 'twas fresh in murmur—as, you know, 32
What great ones do the less will prattle of— 33
That he did seek the love of fair Olivia.

VIOLA What's she?

CAPTAIN
A virtuous maid, the daughter of a count
That died some twelvemonth since, then leaving her
In the protection of his son, her brother,
Who shortly also died; for whose dear love,
They say, she hath abjured the sight
And company of men.

VIOLA   O, that I served that lady,
And might not be delivered to the world 42
Till I had made mine own occasion mellow, 43
What my estate is!

CAPTAIN   That were hard to compass, 44
Because she will admit no kind of suit,
No, not the Duke's.

VIOLA
There is a fair behavior in thee, Captain,
And though that nature with a beauteous wall
Doth oft close in pollution, yet of thee
I will believe thou hast a mind that suits
With this thy fair and outward character. 51
I prithee, and I'll pay thee bounteously,
Conceal me what I am, and be my aid
For such disguise as haply shall become 54
The form of my intent. I'll serve this duke. 55
Thou shalt present me as an eunuch to him. 56
It may be worth thy pains, for I can sing
And speak to him in many sorts of music
That will allow me very worth his service. 59
What else may hap, to time I will commit;
Only shape thou thy silence to my wit. 61

---

32 murmur rumor **33 less** i.e., social inferiors **42 delivered** revealed, made known **43 mellow** ready or convenient (to be made known) **44 estate** position in society. **compass** bring about, encompass **51 character** face or features as indicating moral qualities **54 become** suit **55 form of my intent** nature of my purpose (with suggestion of outward appearance in *form*) **56 eunuch** castrato, high-voiced singer **59 allow me** cause me to be acknowledged **61 wit** plan, invention

CAPTAIN
 Be you his eunuch, and your mute I'll be;
 When my tongue blabs, then let mine eyes not see.
VIOLA I thank thee. Lead me on.   *Exeunt.*

❖

1.3 *Enter Sir Toby [Belch] and Maria.*

SIR TOBY What a plague means my niece to take the
 death of her brother thus? I am sure care's an enemy
 to life.
MARIA By my troth, Sir Toby, you must come in earlier
 o' nights. Your cousin, my lady, takes great exceptions 5
 to your ill hours.
SIR TOBY Why, let her except before excepted.   7
MARIA Ay, but you must confine yourself within the
 modest limits of order.   9
SIR TOBY Confine? I'll confine myself no finer than I am. 10
 These clothes are good enough to drink in, and so be
 these boots too. An they be not, let them hang them- 12
 selves in their own straps.
MARIA That quaffing and drinking will undo you. I
 heard my lady talk of it yesterday, and of a foolish
 knight that you brought in one night here to be her
 wooer.
SIR TOBY Who, Sir Andrew Aguecheek?
MARIA Ay, he.
SIR TOBY He's as tall a man as any's in Illyria.   20
MARIA What's that to the purpose?
SIR TOBY Why, he has three thousand ducats a year.
MARIA Ay, but he'll have but a year in all these ducats. 23
 He's a very fool and a prodigal.
SIR TOBY Fie, that you'll say so! He plays o' the viol-de- 25
 gamboys, and speaks three or four languages word for 26

1.3. Location: Olivia's house.
5 cousin i.e., kinswoman **7 except before excepted** (Plays on the legal
phrase *exceptis excipiendis*, "with the exceptions before named." Sir
Toby means that enough exceptions to his behavior have already been
taken.) **9 modest** moderate **10 confine myself** dress myself (playing
on Maria's use of *confine*, limit). **finer** (1) better (2) tighter **12 An** if
20 tall brave **23 he'll . . . ducats** i.e., he'll spend all his money within a
year **25–26 viol-de-gamboys** viola da gamba, leg-viol, bass viol

word without book, and hath all the good gifts of 27
nature.

MARIA He hath indeed, almost natural, for, besides that 29
he's a fool, he's a great quarreler, and but that he hath
the gift of a coward to allay the gust he hath in quar- 31
reling, 'tis thought among the prudent he would
quickly have the gift of a grave.

SIR TOBY By this hand, they are scoundrels and sub- 34
stractors that say so of him. Who are they?   35

MARIA They that add, moreover, he's drunk nightly in
your company.

SIR TOBY With drinking healths to my niece. I'll drink
to her as long as there is a passage in my throat and
drink in Illyria. He's a coward and a coistrel that will 40
not drink to my niece till his brains turn o' the toe like
a parish top. What, wench? *Castiliano vulgo!* For here 42
comes Sir Andrew Agueface.   43

Enter Sir Andrew [Aguecheek].

SIR ANDREW Sir Toby Belch! How now, Sir Toby Belch?
SIR TOBY Sweet Sir Andrew!
SIR ANDREW Bless you, fair shrew.
MARIA And you too, sir.
SIR TOBY Accost, Sir Andrew, accost.   48
SIR ANDREW What's that?
SIR TOBY My niece's chambermaid.   50
SIR ANDREW Good Mistress Accost, I desire better ac-
quaintance.
MARIA My name is Mary, sir.
SIR ANDREW Good Mistress Mary Accost—

---

27 without book by heart   **29 natural** (with a play on the sense "born
idiot")   **31 allay the gust** moderate the taste   **34–35 substractors** i.e.,
detractors   **40 coistrel** horse-groom, base fellow   **42 parish top** a large
top provided by the parish to be spun by whipping, apparently for
exercise in cold weather.   **Castiliano vulgo** (Of uncertain meaning.
Castilians were noted for their decorum, and possibly Sir Toby is urging
Maria to behave politely to Sir Andrew.)   **43 Agueface** (Like *Aguecheek*,
this name betokens the thin, pale countenance of one suffering from an
ague.)   **48 Accost** go alongside (a nautical term), i.e., greet her, address
her   **50 chambermaid** lady in waiting (a gentlewoman, not one who
would do menial tasks)

SIR TOBY You mistake, knight. "Accost" is front her,
board her, woo her, assail her.   56
SIR ANDREW By my troth, I would not undertake her in
this company. Is that the meaning of "accost"?
MARIA Fare you well, gentlemen.   [*Going.*]
SIR TOBY An thou let part so, Sir Andrew, would thou   60
mightst never draw sword again.
SIR ANDREW An you part so, mistress, I would I might
never draw sword again. Fair lady, do you think you
have fools in hand?   64
MARIA Sir, I have not you by the hand.
SIR ANDREW Marry, but you shall have, and here's my   66
hand.
MARIA Now, sir, thought is free. I pray you, bring your 68
hand to the buttery-bar, and let it drink.   69
SIR ANDREW Wherefore, sweetheart? What's your met-
aphor?
MARIA It's dry, sir.   72
SIR ANDREW Why, I think so. I am not such an ass but
I can keep my hand dry. But what's your jest?
MARIA A dry jest, sir.   75
SIR ANDREW Are you full of them?
MARIA Ay, sir, I have them at my fingers' ends. Marry,
now I let go your hand, I am barren.   *Exit Maria.* 78
SIR TOBY O knight, thou lack'st a cup of canary! When   79
did I see thee so put down?
SIR ANDREW Never in your life, I think, unless you see
canary put me down. Methinks sometimes I have no
more wit than a Christian or an ordinary man has. But
I am a great eater of beef, and I believe that does harm
to my wit.
SIR TOBY No question.

---

56 board greet, approach (as though preparing to board in a naval
encounter) **60 An . . . part** if you let her leave **64 have . . . hand** i.e.,
have to deal with fools. (But Maria puns on the literal sense.) **66 Marry**
i.e., indeed. (Originally, "By the Virgin Mary.") **68 thought is free** i.e., I
may think what I like. (Proverbial; replying to *do you think . . . in hand*,
above.) **69 buttery-bar** ledge on top of the half-door to the buttery or
wine cellar **72 dry** thirsty; also dried up, a sign of age and debility
75 dry (1) ironic (2) dull, barren (referring to Sir Andrew) **78 barren** i.e.,
barren of jests and of Andrew's hand **79 canary** a sweet wine from the
Canary Islands

SIR ANDREW An I thought that, I'd forswear it. I'll ride
home tomorrow, Sir Toby.

SIR TOBY *Pourquoi*, my dear knight?　　　　　89

SIR ANDREW What is *"pourquoi"*? Do or not do? I
would I had bestowed that time in the tongues that I　91
have in fencing, dancing, and bearbaiting. O, had I
but followed the arts!　　　　　93

SIR TOBY Then hadst thou had an excellent head of hair.

SIR ANDREW Why, would that have mended my hair?　　95

SIR TOBY Past question, for thou seest it will not curl by
nature.

SIR ANDREW But it becomes me well enough, does 't
not?

SIR TOBY Excellent. It hangs like flax on a distaff, and I　100
hope to see a huswife take thee between her legs and
spin it off.　　　　　102

SIR ANDREW Faith, I'll home tomorrow, Sir Toby. Your
niece will not be seen, or if she be, it's four to one
she'll none of me. The Count himself here hard by　105
woos her.

SIR TOBY She'll none o' the Count. She'll not match
above her degree, neither in estate, years, nor wit; I　108
have heard her swear 't. Tut, there's life in 't, man.　109

SIR ANDREW I'll stay a month longer. I am a fellow o' the
strangest mind i' the world; I delight in masques and
revels sometimes altogether.

SIR TOBY Art thou good at these kickshawses, knight?　113

SIR ANDREW As any man in Illyria, whatsoever he be,
under the degree of my betters, and yet I will not com-　115
pare with an old man.　　　　　116

SIR TOBY What is thy excellence in a galliard, knight?　117

---

89 Pourquoi why **91 tongues** languages. (Perhaps also suggests *tongs*,
curling irons.) **93 the arts** the liberal arts, learning. (But Sir Toby plays
on the phrase as meaning "artifice," the antithesis of *nature*.) **95 mended**
improved **100 distaff** a staff for holding the flax, tow, or wool in
spinning **102 spin it off** i.e., cause you to lose hair as a result of vene-
real disease, gotten from the *huswife* (suggesting *hussy*, "whore")
105 Count i.e., Duke Orsino, sometimes referred to as Count. **hard**
near **108 degree** social position. **estate** fortune, social position
109 there's life in 't i.e., while there's life there's hope **113 kickshawses** delicacies, fancy trifles. (From the French, *quelque chose*.)
115 under . . . betters excepting those who are above me **116 old
man** experienced person (?) **117 galliard** lively dance in triple time

SIR ANDREW   Faith, I can cut a caper.   118
SIR TOBY   And I can cut the mutton to 't.
SIR ANDREW   And I think I have the back-trick simply as 120
  strong as any man in Illyria.
SIR TOBY   Wherefore are these things hid? Wherefore have
  these gifts a curtain before 'em? Are they like to 123
  take dust, like Mistress Mall's picture? Why dost thou 124
  not go to church in a galliard and come home in a
  coranto? My very walk should be a jig; I would not so 126
  much as make water but in a sink-a-pace. What dost 127
  thou mean? Is it a world to hide virtues in? I did think, 128
  by the excellent constitution of thy leg, it was formed
  under the star of a galliard.   130
SIR ANDREW   Ay, 'tis strong, and it does indifferent well 131
  in a dun-colored stock. Shall we set about some re- 132
  vels?
SIR TOBY   What shall we do else? Were we not born under Taurus?   135
SIR ANDREW   Taurus? That's sides and heart.
SIR TOBY   No, sir, it is legs and thighs. Let me see thee
  caper. Ha, higher! Ha, ha, excellent!
                      [*Sir Andrew capers.*] *Exeunt.*

❖

1.4   *Enter Valentine, and Viola in man's attire.*

VALENTINE   If the Duke continue these favors towards
  you, Cesario, you are like to be much advanced. He
  hath known you but three days, and already you are
  no stranger.

---

118 cut a caper make a lively leap. (But Sir Toby puns on the *caper* used
to make a sauce served with mutton. *Mutton* in turn suggests "whore.")
120 back-trick backward step in the galliard   **123–124 like to take**
likely to collect   **124 Mistress Mall's picture** i.e., perhaps the portrait
of some woman protected from light and dust, as many pictures were,
by curtains   **126 coranto** lively running dance   **127 sink-a-pace** dance
like the galliard. (French *cinquepace*.)   **128 virtues** talents   **130 under
. . . galliard** i.e., under a star favorable to dancing   **131 indifferent**
moderately   **132 stock** stocking   **135 Taurus** zodiacal sign. (Sir Andrew
is mistaken, since Leo governed sides and hearts in medical astrology.
Taurus governed legs and thighs, or, more commonly, neck and throat.)

1.4. Location: Orsino's court.

VIOLA   You either fear his humor or my negligence, that 5
  you call in question the continuance of his love. Is he
  inconstant, sir, in his favors?
VALENTINE   No, believe me.

Enter Duke [Orsino], Curio, and attendants.

VIOLA   I thank you. Here comes the Count.
ORSINO   Who saw Cesario, ho?
VIOLA   On your attendance, my lord, here.
ORSINO
  Stand you awhile aloof. [*The others stand aside.*]
    Cesario,
  Thou know'st no less but all. I have unclasped
  To thee the book even of my secret soul.
  Therefore, good youth, address thy gait unto her;   15
  Be not denied access, stand at her doors,
  And tell them, there thy fixèd foot shall grow   17
  Till thou have audience.
VIOLA   Sure, my noble lord,
  If she be so abandoned to her sorrow
  As it is spoke, she never will admit me.
ORSINO
  Be clamorous and leap all civil bounds   21
  Rather than make unprofited return.
VIOLA
  Say I do speak with her, my lord, what then?
ORSINO
  O, then unfold the passion of my love;
  Surprise her with discourse of my dear faith.   25
  It shall become thee well to act my woes;   26
  She will attend it better in thy youth
  Than in a nuncio's of more grave aspect.   28
VIOLA
  I think not so, my lord.
ORSINO   Dear lad, believe it;
  For they shall yet belie thy happy years
  That say thou art a man. Diana's lip

---

5 humor changeableness   **15 address thy gait** go   **17 them** i.e., Olivia's
servants   **21 civil bounds** bounds of civility   **25 Surprise** take by storm.
(A military term.)   **26 become** suit   **28 nuncio's** messenger's

Is not more smooth and rubious; thy small pipe　　32
Is as the maiden's organ, shrill and sound,　　33
And all is semblative a woman's part.　　34
I know thy constellation is right apt　　35
For this affair.—Some four or five attend him;
All, if you will, for I myself am best
When least in company.—Prosper well in this,
And thou shalt live as freely as thy lord,
To call his fortunes thine.

VIOLA　　　　　　　　　I'll do my best
To woo your lady. [*Aside.*] Yet a barful strife!　　41
Whoe'er I woo, myself would be his wife.　　　　*Exeunt.*

✤

1.5　　*Enter Maria and Clown [Feste].*

MARIA　Nay, either tell me where thou hast been, or I
will not open my lips so wide as a bristle may enter in
way of thy excuse. My lady will hang thee for thy ab-
sence.

FESTE　Let her hang me. He that is well hanged in this
world needs to fear no colors.　　6

MARIA　Make that good.　　7

FESTE　He shall see none to fear.

MARIA　A good lenten answer. I can tell thee where that　9
saying was born, of "I fear no colors."

FESTE　Where, good Mistress Mary?

MARIA　In the wars, and that may you be bold to say in　12
your foolery.

FESTE　Well, God give them wisdom that have it; and
those that are fools, let them use their talents.　　15

---

32 rubious ruby red.　**pipe** voice, throat　**33 shrill and sound** high and
clear, uncracked　**34 semblative** resembling, like　**35 constellation** i.e.,
nature as determined by your horoscope　**41 barful strife** endeavor full
of impediments

1.5. Location: Olivia's house.
6 fear no colors i.e., fear no foe, fear nothing (with pun on *colors*,
worldly deceptions, and *collars*, halters or nooses)　**7 Make that good**
explain that　**9 lenten** meager, scanty (like lenten fare)　**12 In the wars**
(where *colors* would mean "military standards")　**15 talents** abilities
(also alluding to the parable of the talents, Matthew 25:14–29)

MARIA   Yet you will be hanged for being so long absent;
or to be turned away, is not that as good as a hanging 17
to you?

FESTE Many a good hanging prevents a bad marriage;
and for turning away, let summer bear it out.   20

MARIA   You are resolute, then?

FESTE Not so, neither, but I am resolved on two
points.   23

MARIA   That if one break, the other will hold; or if both
break, your gaskins fall.   25

FESTE Apt, in good faith, very apt. Well, go thy way;
if Sir Toby would leave drinking, thou wert as witty a 27
piece of Eve's flesh as any in Illyria.   28

MARIA   Peace, you rogue, no more o' that. Here comes
my lady. Make your excuse wisely, you were best.   30

[Exit.]

Enter Lady Olivia with Malvolio [and attendants].

FESTE Wit, an 't be thy will, put me into good fooling! 31
Those wits that think they have thee do very oft prove
fools, and I that am sure I lack thee may pass for a wise
man. For what says Quinapalus? "Better a witty fool 34
than a foolish wit."—God bless thee, lady!

OLIVIA   Take the fool away.

FESTE Do you not hear, fellows? Take away the lady.

OLIVIA   Go to, you're a dry fool. I'll no more of you. Be- 38
sides, you grow dishonest.   39

FESTE Two faults, madonna, that drink and good 40
counsel will amend. For give the dry fool drink, then
is the fool not dry. Bid the dishonest man mend himself; if he mend, he is no longer dishonest; if he cannot, let the botcher mend him. Anything that's 44

---

17 turned away dismissed (possibly also meaning "turned off,"
"hanged") **20 for** as for. **let . . . out** i.e., let mild weather make dis-
missal endurable **23 points** (Maria plays on the meaning "laces used to
hold up hose or breeches.") **25 gaskins** wide breeches **27–28 thou . . .
Illyria** (Feste may be observing ironically that Maria is as likely to prove
witty as Sir Toby is to give up drinking; or he may hint at a match
between the two.) **30 you were best** it would be best for you **31 an 't**
if it **34 Quinapalus** (Feste's invented authority.) **38 dry** dull **39 dishonest** unreliable; wicked **40 madonna** my lady **44 botcher** mender of
old clothes and shoes

mended is but patched; virtue that transgresses is but patched with sin, and sin that amends is but patched with virtue. If that this simple syllogism will serve, so; if it will not, what remedy? As there is no true cuckold 48 but calamity, so beauty's a flower. The lady bade take 49 away the fool; therefore I say again, take her away.

OLIVIA   Sir, I bade them take away you.

FESTE   Misprision in the highest degree! Lady, *cucul-* 52 *lus non facit monachum;* that's as much to say as I 53 wear not motley in my brain. Good madonna, give me 54 leave to prove you a fool.

OLIVIA   Can you do it?

FESTE   Dexterously, good madonna.

OLIVIA   Make your proof.

FESTE   I must catechize you for it, madonna. Good my 59 mouse of virtue, answer me.   60

OLIVIA   Well, sir, for want of other idleness, I'll bide 61 your proof.

FESTE   Good madonna, why mourn'st thou?

OLIVIA   Good Fool, for my brother's death.

FESTE   I think his soul is in hell, madonna.

OLIVIA   I know his soul is in heaven, Fool.

FESTE   The more fool, madonna, to mourn for your brother's soul, being in heaven. Take away the fool, gentlemen.

OLIVIA   What think you of this fool, Malvolio? Doth he not mend?   71

MALVOLIO   Yes, and shall do till the pangs of death shake him. Infirmity, that decays the wise, doth ever make the better fool.

FESTE   God send you, sir, a speedy infirmity, for the better increasing your folly! Sir Toby will be sworn that I am no fox, but he will not pass his word for two-pence that you are no fool.

48–49 As . . . flower i.e., Olivia has wedded calamity but will not be faithful to it, for the natural course is to seize the moment of youth and beauty before we lose it   **52 Misprision** mistake, misunderstanding (a legal term meaning a wrongful action or misdemeanor)   **52–53 cucullus . . . monachum** the cowl does not make the monk   **54 motley** the many-colored garment of jesters   **59–60 Good . . . virtue** my good virtuous mouse. (A term of endearment.)   **61 idleness** pastime.   **bide** endure   **71 mend** i.e., improve, grow more amusing. (But Malvolio uses the word to mean "grow more like a fool.")

OLIVIA   How say you to that, Malvolio?

MALVOLIO   I marvel your ladyship takes delight in such
a barren rascal. I saw him put down the other day with 81
an ordinary fool that has no more brain than a stone.
Look you now, he's out of his guard already. Unless 83
you laugh and minister occasion to him, he is gagged. 84
I protest I take these wise men that crow so at these set 85
kind of fools no better than the fools' zanies. 86

OLIVIA   O, you are sick of self-love, Malvolio, and taste
with a distempered appetite. To be generous, guiltless,
and of free disposition is to take those things for bird- 89
bolts that you deem cannon bullets. There is no slan- 90
der in an allowed fool, though he do nothing but rail; 91
nor no railing in a known discreet man, though he do
nothing but reprove.

FESTE   Now Mercury endue thee with leasing, for 94
thou speak'st well of fools!

   Enter Maria.

MARIA   Madam, there is at the gate a young gentleman
much desires to speak with you.

OLIVIA   From the Count Orsino, is it?

MARIA   I know not, madam. 'Tis a fair young man, and
well attended.

OLIVIA   Who of my people hold him in delay?

MARIA   Sir Toby, madam, your kinsman.

OLIVIA   Fetch him off, I pray you. He speaks nothing
but madman. Fie on him! [*Exit Maria.*] Go you, Mal- 104
volio. If it be a suit from the Count, I am sick, or not at
home; what you will, to dismiss it. (*Exit Malvolio.*)
Now you see, sir, how your fooling grows old, and 107
people dislike it.

FESTE   Thou hast spoke for us, madonna, as if thy eld-
est son should be a fool; whose skull Jove cram with
brains, for—here he comes—

---

81 with by   **83 out of his guard** defenseless, unprovided with a witty
answer   **84 minister occasion** provide opportunity (for his fooling)
85 protest avow, declare.   **crow** laugh stridently.   **set** artificial, stereo-
typed   **86 zanies** assistants, aping attendants   **89 free** magnanimous
89–90 bird-bolts blunt arrows for shooting small birds   **91 allowed**
licensed (to speak freely)   **94 Now . . . leasing** i.e., may Mercury, the god
of deception, make you a skillful liar   **104 madman** i.e., the words of
madness   **107 old** stale

Enter Sir Toby.

one of thy kin has a most weak *pia mater*.   112

OLIVIA   By mine honor, half drunk. What is he at the gate, cousin?

SIR TOBY   A gentleman.

OLIVIA   A gentleman? What gentleman?

SIR TOBY   'Tis a gentleman here—[*He belches.*] A plague o' these pickle-herring! How now, sot?   118

FESTE   Good Sir Toby.

OLIVIA   Cousin, cousin, how have you come so early by this lethargy?

SIR TOBY   Lechery? I defy lechery. There's one at the gate.

OLIVIA   Ay, marry, what is he?

SIR TOBY   Let him be the devil, an he will, I care not. Give me faith, say I. Well, it's all one.   *Exit.* 126

OLIVIA   What's a drunken man like, Fool?

FESTE   Like a drowned man, a fool, and a madman. One draft above heat makes him a fool, the second 129 mads him, and a third drowns him.

OLIVIA   Go thou and seek the crowner, and let him sit 131 o' my coz; for he's in the third degree of drink, he's 132 drowned. Go, look after him.

FESTE   He is but mad yet, madonna; and the fool shall look to the madman.   [*Exit.*]

Enter Malvolio.

MALVOLIO   Madam, yond young fellow swears he will speak with you. I told him you were sick; he takes on him to understand so much, and therefore comes to speak with you. I told him you were asleep; he seems to have a foreknowledge of that too, and therefore comes to speak with you. What is to be said to him, lady? He's fortified against any denial.

OLIVIA   Tell him he shall not speak with me.

MALVOLIO   He's been told so; and he says he'll stand at

---

112 pia mater i.e., brain (actually the soft membrane enclosing the brain)   **118 sot** (1) fool (2) drunkard   **126 Give me faith** i.e., to resist the devil.   **it's all one** it doesn't matter   **129 draft** drinking portion.   **above heat** above the point needed to make him normally warm   **131 crowner** coroner   **131–132 sit o' my coz** hold an inquest on my kinsman (Sir Toby)

your door like a sheriff's post, and be the supporter to 145
a bench, but he'll speak with you.

OLIVIA   What kind o' man is he?

MALVOLIO   Why, of mankind.

OLIVIA   What manner of man?

MALVOLIO   Of very ill manner. He'll speak with you,
will you or no.

OLIVIA   Of what personage and years is he?

MALVOLIO   Not yet old enough for a man, nor young
enough for a boy; as a squash is before 'tis a peascod, 154
or a codling when 'tis almost an apple. 'Tis with him 155
in standing water, between boy and man. He is very 156
well-favored and he speaks very shrewishly. One 157
would think his mother's milk were scarce out
of him.

OLIVIA   Let him approach. Call in my gentlewoman.

MALVOLIO   Gentlewoman, my lady calls.   *Exit.*

    Enter Maria.

OLIVIA
Give me my veil. Come, throw it o'er my face.
We'll once more hear Orsino's embassy.

                              [*Olivia veils.*]

    Enter Viola.

VIOLA   The honorable lady of the house, which is she?

OLIVIA   Speak to me; I shall answer for her. Your will?

VIOLA   Most radiant, exquisite, and unmatchable
beauty—I pray you, tell me if this be the lady of the
house, for I never saw her. I would be loath to cast
away my speech; for besides that it is excellently well
penned, I have taken great pains to con it. Good beau- 170
ties, let me sustain no scorn; I am very comptible, even 171
to the least sinister usage. 172

OLIVIA   Whence came you, sir?

VIOLA   I can say little more than I have studied, and that

---

145 sheriff's post post before the sheriff's door on which proclamations
and notices were fixed   **154 squash** unripe pea pod.   **peascod** pea pod
155 codling unripe apple   **156 in standing water** at the turn of the
tide   **157 well-favored** good-looking.   **shrewishly** sharply   **170 con**
learn by heart   **171 comptible** susceptible, sensitive   **172 least sinister**
slightest discourteous

question's out of my part. Good gentle one, give me
modest assurance if you be the lady of the house, that 176
I may proceed in my speech.

OLIVIA Are you a comedian? 178

VIOLA No, my profound heart; and yet, by the very 179
fangs of malice, I swear I am not that I play. Are you
the lady of the house?

OLIVIA If I do not usurp myself, I am. 182

VIOLA Most certain, if you are she, you do usurp your- 183
self; for what is yours to bestow is not yours to reserve. 184
But this is from my commission. I will on with my 185
speech in your praise, and then show you the heart of
my message.

OLIVIA Come to what is important in 't. I forgive you 188
the praise.

VIOLA Alas, I took great pains to study it, and 'tis poetical.

OLIVIA It is the more like to be feigned. I pray you, keep
it in. I heard you were saucy at my gates, and allowed
your approach rather to wonder at you than to hear
you. If you be not mad, begone; if you have reason, 195
be brief. 'Tis not that time of moon with me to make 196
one in so skipping a dialogue. 197

MARIA Will you hoist sail, sir? Here lies your way.

VIOLA No, good swabber, I am to hull here a little 199
longer.—Some mollification for your giant, sweet lady. 200
Tell me your mind; I am a messenger.

OLIVIA Sure you have some hideous matter to deliver,
when the courtesy of it is so fearful. Speak your office. 203

VIOLA It alone concerns your ear. I bring no overture of

---

176 modest reasonable   **178 comedian** actor   **179 profound** very wise,
figuratively deep   **182 do . . . myself** am not an impostor   **183–184 usurp
yourself** i.e., betray yourself, by withholding yourself from Orsino
185 from outside of   **188 forgive you** excuse you from repeating   **195 If
. . . mad** i.e., if you don't have madness to excuse your saucy behavior (?)
Possibly an error for *If . . . but mad* (?)   **reason** sanity   **196 moon** (The
moon was thought to affect lunatics according to its changing phases.)
196–197 make one take part   **199 swabber** one in charge of washing
the decks. (A nautical retort to *hoist sail*.)   **hull** lie with sails furled
200 Some . . . for i.e., please mollify, pacify.   **giant** i.e., the diminutive
Maria who, like many giants in medieval romances, is guarding the
lady   **203 courtesy** i.e., introduction.   **office** commission

war, no taxation of homage. I hold the olive in my 205
hand; my words are as full of peace as matter.

OLIVIA Yet you began rudely. What are you? What
would you?

VIOLA The rudeness that hath appeared in me have I
learned from my entertainment. What I am, and what 210
I would, are as secret as maidenhead—to your ears,
divinity; to any other's, profanation.

OLIVIA Give us the place alone; we will hear this divinity. [*Exeunt Maria and attendants.*] Now, sir, what is
your text?

VIOLA Most sweet lady—

OLIVIA A comfortable doctrine, and much may be said 217
of it. Where lies your text?

VIOLA In Orsino's bosom.

OLIVIA In his bosom? In what chapter of his bosom?

VIOLA To answer by the method, in the first of his 221
heart.

OLIVIA O, I have read it; it is heresy. Have you no more
to say?

VIOLA Good madam, let me see your face.

OLIVIA Have you any commission from your lord to ne-
gotiate with my face? You are now out of your text.
But we will draw the curtain and show you the picture. [*Unveiling.*] Look you, sir, such a one I was this 229
present. Is 't not well done? 230

VIOLA Excellently done, if God did all.

OLIVIA 'Tis in grain, sir; 'twill endure wind and 232
weather.

VIOLA

'Tis beauty truly blent, whose red and white 234
Nature's own sweet and cunning hand laid on. 235
Lady, you are the cruel'st she alive
If you will lead these graces to the grave
And leave the world no copy. 238

---

205 taxation demand for the payment   **210 entertainment** reception
217 comfortable comforting   **221 To . . . method** i.e., to continue the
metaphor (of delivering a sermon, begun with *divinity* and *what is your
text* and continued in *doctrine, heresy,* etc.)   **229–230 this present** at this
present time. (Since it was customary to hang curtains in front of pictures,
Olivia in unveiling speaks as if she were displaying a picture of herself.)
232 in grain fast dyed   **234 blent** blended   **235 cunning** skillful   **238 copy**
i.e., a child. (But Olivia uses the word to mean "transcript.")

OLIVIA   O, sir, I will not be so hardhearted. I will give
out divers schedules of my beauty. It shall be inven- 240
toried, and every particle and utensil labeled to my will: 241
as, item, two lips, indifferent red; item, two gray eyes, 242
with lids to them; item, one neck, one chin, and so
forth. Were you sent hither to praise me?   244

VIOLA
  I see you what you are, you are too proud;
  But, if you were the devil, you are fair.   246
  My lord and master loves you. O, such love
  Could be but recompensed, though you were crowned 248
  The nonpareil of beauty!

OLIVIA   How does he love me?

VIOLA
  With adorations, fertile tears,   250
  With groans that thunder love, with sighs of fire.

OLIVIA
  Your lord does know my mind; I cannot love him.
  Yet I suppose him virtuous, know him noble,
  Of great estate, of fresh and stainless youth;
  In voices well divulged, free, learned, and valiant,   255
  And in dimension and the shape of nature
  A gracious person. But yet I cannot love him.   257
  He might have took his answer long ago.

VIOLA
  If I did love you in my master's flame,   259
  With such a suffering, such a deadly life,   260
  In your denial I would find no sense;
  I would not understand it.

OLIVIA   Why, what would you?

VIOLA
  Make me a willow cabin at your gate,   263
  And call upon my soul within the house;   264
  Write loyal cantons of contemnèd love,   265

240 schedules inventories   **241 utensil** article, item.   **labeled** added as
a codicil   **242 indifferent** somewhat   **244 praise** appraise   **246 if** even
if   **248 but . . . though** no more than evenly repaid even though
250 fertile copious   **255 In . . . divulged** well reported in public opinion.   **free** generous   **257 gracious** graceful, attractive   **259 flame**
passion   **260 deadly** deathlike   **263 willow cabin** shelter, hut. (Willow
was a symbol of unrequited love.)   **264 my soul** i.e., Olivia   **265 cantons**
songs.   **contemnèd** rejected

And sing them loud even in the dead of night;
Hallow your name to the reverberate hills,   267
And make the babbling gossip of the air   268
Cry out "Olivia!" O, you should not rest
Between the elements of air and earth
But you should pity me!

OLIVIA   You might do much.
What is your parentage?

VIOLA
Above my fortunes, yet my state is well: 273
I am a gentleman.

OLIVIA   Get you to your lord.
I cannot love him. Let him send no more—
Unless, perchance, you come to me again
To tell me how he takes it. Fare you well.
I thank you for your pains. Spend this for me.
                          [*She offers a purse.*]

VIOLA
I am no fee'd post, lady; keep your purse.   279
My master, not myself, lacks recompense.
Love make his heart of flint that you shall love, 281
And let your fervor, like my master's, be
Placed in contempt! Farewell, fair cruelty.   *Exit.*

OLIVIA   "What is your parentage?"
"Above my fortunes, yet my state is well:
I am a gentleman." I'll be sworn thou art!
Thy tongue, thy face, thy limbs, actions, and spirit
Do give thee fivefold blazon. Not too fast! Soft, soft! 288
Unless the master were the man. How now?
Even so quickly may one catch the plague?
Methinks I feel this youth's perfections
With an invisible and subtle stealth
To creep in at mine eyes. Well, let it be.
What ho, Malvolio!

        Enter Malvolio.

MALVOLIO   Here, madam, at your service.

---

267 Hallow (1) halloo (2) bless   **268 babbling ... air** echo   **273 state** social standing   **279 fee'd post** messenger to be tipped   **281 Love ... love** may Love make the heart of the man you love as hard as flint   **288 blazon** heraldic description

OLIVIA
　Run after that same peevish messenger,
　The County's man. He left this ring behind him,　　296
　　　　　　　　　　[*Giving a ring*]
　Would I or not. Tell him I'll none of it.　　297
　Desire him not to flatter with his lord,　　298
　Nor hold him up with hopes; I am not for him.
　If that the youth will come this way tomorrow,
　I'll give him reasons for 't. Hie thee, Malvolio.
MALVOLIO　Madam, I will.　　　　　　　　*Exit.*
OLIVIA
　I do I know not what, and fear to find
　Mine eye too great a flatterer for my mind.　　304
　Fate, show thy force. Ourselves we do not owe;　　305
　What is decreed must be, and be this so.　　[*Exit.*]

❖

2.1 *Enter Antonio and Sebastian.*

ANTONIO Will you stay no longer? Nor will you not that 1
I go with you?

SEBASTIAN By your patience, no. My stars shine darkly 3
over me. The malignancy of my fate might perhaps 4
distemper yours; therefore I shall crave of you your 5
leave, that I may bear my evils alone. It were a bad
recompense for your love to lay any of them on you.

ANTONIO Let me yet know of you whither you are
bound.

SEBASTIAN No, sooth, sir; my determinate voyage is 10
mere extravagancy. But I perceive in you so excellent 11
a touch of modesty that you will not extort from me
what I am willing to keep in; therefore it charges me 13
in manners the rather to express myself. You must 14
know of me then, Antonio, my name is Sebastian,
which I called Roderigo. My father was that Sebastian
of Messaline whom I know you have heard of. He left 17
behind him myself and a sister, both born in an hour. 18
If the heavens had been pleased, would we had so
ended! But you, sir, altered that, for some hour before 20
you took me from the breach of the sea was my sister 21
drowned.

ANTONIO Alas the day!

SEBASTIAN A lady, sir, though it was said she much resembled me, was yet of many accounted beautiful. But
though I could not with such estimable wonder over- 26
far believe that, yet thus far I will boldly publish her: 27
she bore a mind that envy could not but call fair. She
is drowned already, sir, with salt water, though I seem
to drown her remembrance again with more.

2.1. Location: Somewhere in Illyria.
1 Nor will you not do you not wish   **3 patience** leave   **4 malignancy**
malevolence (of the stars; also in a medical sense)   **5 distemper** disor-
der, disturb   **10 sooth** truly.   **determinate** intended, determined upon
11 extravagancy aimless wandering   **13 am willing . . . in** wish to keep
secret   **13–14 it . . . manners** it is incumbent upon me in all courtesy
14 express reveal   **17 Messaline** probably Messina, or, more likely,
Massila (the modern Marseilles). In Plautus' *Menaechmi*, Massilians and
Illyrians are mentioned together.   **18 in an hour** in the same hour
20 some hour about an hour   **21 breach of the sea** surf   **26 estimable
wonder** admiring judgment   **27 publish** proclaim

ANTONIO Pardon me, sir, your bad entertainment. 31

SEBASTIAN O good Antonio, forgive me your trouble. 32

ANTONIO If you will not murder me for my love, let me 33
be your servant.

SEBASTIAN If you will not undo what you have done,
that is, kill him whom you have recovered, desire it 36
not. Fare ye well at once. My bosom is full of kindness, 37
and I am yet so near the manners of my mother that 38
upon the least occasion more mine eyes will tell tales
of me. I am bound to the Count Orsino's court. Farewell.   *Exit.*

ANTONIO
The gentleness of all the gods go with thee!
I have many enemies in Orsino's court,
Else would I very shortly see thee there.
But come what may, I do adore thee so
That danger shall seem sport, and I will go.   *Exit.*

❖

2.2 *Enter Viola and Malvolio, at several doors.*

MALVOLIO Were not you even now with the Countess
Olivia?

VIOLA Even now, sir. On a moderate pace I have since
arrived but hither.

MALVOLIO She returns this ring to you, sir. You might
have saved me my pains, to have taken it away yourself. She adds, moreover, that you should put your
lord into a desperate assurance she will none of him. 8
And one thing more, that you be never so hardy to 9
come again in his affairs, unless it be to report your
lord's taking of this. Receive it so.

VIOLA She took the ring of me. I'll none of it. 12

---

31 entertainment reception, hospitality **32 your trouble** the trouble
I put you to **33 murder me for** i.e., be the cause of my death in
return for **36 recovered** rescued, restored **37 kindness** tenderness,
natural emotion (of grief) **38 manners of my mother** womanish
qualities

2.2. Location: Outside Olivia's house.
s.d. several different **8 desperate** without hope **9 hardy** bold **12 She
. . . it** (Viola tells a quick and friendly lie to shield Olivia.)

MALVOLIO Come, sir, you peevishly threw it to her, and
her will is it should be so returned. [*He throws down
the ring.*] If it be worth stooping for, there it lies, in 15
your eye; if not, be it his that finds it.　　　　*Exit.* 16

VIOLA [*Picking up the ring*]
I left no ring with her. What means this lady?
Fortune forbid my outside have not charmed her!
She made good view of me, indeed so much　　　　19
That sure methought her eyes had lost her tongue,　20
For she did speak in starts distractedly.
She loves me, sure! The cunning of her passion
Invites me in this churlish messenger.　　　　　23
None of my lord's ring? Why, he sent her none.
I am the man. If it be so—as 'tis—
Poor lady, she were better love a dream.
Disguise, I see, thou art a wickedness
Wherein the pregnant enemy does much.　　　　28
How easy is it for the proper false　　　　　　29
In women's waxen hearts to set their forms!　　30
Alas, our frailty is the cause, not we,
For such as we are made of, such we be.　　　　32
How will this fadge? My master loves her dearly,　33
And I, poor monster, fond as much on him;　　　34
And she, mistaken, seems to dote on me.
What will become of this? As I am man,
My state is desperate for my master's love;
As I am woman—now, alas the day!—
What thriftless sighs shall poor Olivia breathe!　　39
O Time, thou must untangle this, not I;
It is too hard a knot for me t' untie.　　　　[*Exit.*]

❖

15–16 in your eye in plain sight　**19 made good view of** took a careful
look at　**20 lost** caused her to lose; or, ruined　**23 Invites** tries to
attract　**28 pregnant** quick, resourceful.　**enemy** i.e., Satan　**29 proper
false** men who are handsome and deceitful　**30 waxen** i.e., malleable,
impressionable.　**set their forms** stamp their images (as of a seal)
32 such as . . . of i.e., feminine frailty　**33 fadge** turn out　**34 monster**
i.e., being both man and woman.　**fond** dote　**39 thriftless** unprofitable

2.3   *Enter Sir Toby and Sir Andrew.*

SIR TOBY   Approach, Sir Andrew. Not to be abed after
midnight is to be up betimes; and *diluculo surgere,* 2
thou know'st—

SIR ANDREW   Nay, by my troth, I know not, but I know
to be up late is to be up late.

SIR TOBY   A false conclusion. I hate it as an unfilled can. 6
To be up after midnight and to go to bed then, is early;
so that to go to bed after midnight is to go to bed
betimes. Does not our lives consist of the four ele- 9
ments?   10

SIR ANDREW   Faith, so they say, but I think it rather con-
sists of eating and drinking.

SIR TOBY   Thou'rt a scholar; let us therefore eat and
drink. Marian, I say, a stoup of wine!   14

     Enter Clown [Feste].

SIR ANDREW   Here comes the Fool, i' faith.

FESTE   How now, my hearts! Did you never see the
picture of "we three"?   17

SIR TOBY   Welcome, ass. Now let's have a catch.   18

SIR ANDREW   By my troth, the Fool has an excellent
breast. I had rather than forty shillings I had such a 20
leg, and so sweet a breath to sing, as the Fool has. In
sooth, thou wast in very gracious fooling last night,
when thou spok'st of Pigrogromitus, of the Vapians 23
passing the equinoctial of Queubus. 'Twas very good, 24
i' faith. I sent thee sixpence for thy leman. Hadst it? 25

FESTE   I did impeticos thy gratillity; for Malvolio's 26
nose is no whipstock. My lady has a white hand, and 27

2.3. Location: Olivia's house.
2 betimes early.   **diluculo surgere [saluberrimum est]** to rise early is most
healthful. (A sentence from Lilly's *Latin Grammar*.)   **6 can** tankard
9–10 four elements i.e., fire, air, water, and earth, the elements that were
thought to make up all matter   **14 stoup** drinking vessel   **17 picture of
"we three"** picture of two fools or asses inscribed "we three," the specta-
tor being the third   **18 catch** round   **20 breast** voice   **23–24 Pigrogromitus
. . . Queubus** (Feste's mock erudition.)   **25 leman** sweetheart   **26 impeticos
thy gratillity** (Suggests "impetticoat, or pocket up, thy gratuity.")
27 whipstock whip handle. (Possibly suggests that Malvolio is not very
formidable as overseer in Olivia's household; or, just nonsense.)   **has a
white hand** i.e., is ladylike. (But Feste's speech may be mere nonsense.)

the Myrmidons are no bottle-ale houses.   28

SIR ANDREW Excellent! Why, this is the best fooling,
when all is done. Now, a song.

SIR TOBY Come on, there is sixpence for you. [*He gives
money.*] Let's have a song.

SIR ANDREW There's a testril of me too. [*He gives money.*] 33
If one knight give a—

FESTE Would you have a love song, or a song of good 35
life?   36

SIR TOBY A love song, a love song.

SIR ANDREW Ay, ay, I care not for good life.

FESTE (*Sings*)
    O mistress mine, where are you roaming?
    O, stay and hear, your true love's coming,
        That can sing both high and low.
    Trip no further, pretty sweeting;
    Journeys end in lovers meeting,
        Every wise man's son doth know.

SIR ANDREW Excellent good, i' faith.

SIR TOBY Good, good.

FESTE [*Sings*]
    What is love? 'tis not hereafter;
    Present mirth hath present laughter;
        What's to come is still unsure.
    In delay there lies no plenty,
    Then come kiss me, sweet and twenty;   51
        Youth's a stuff will not endure.

SIR ANDREW A mellifluous voice, as I am true knight.

SIR TOBY A contagious breath.

SIR ANDREW Very sweet and contagious, i' faith.

SIR TOBY To hear by the nose, it is dulcet in contagion. 56
But shall we make the welkin dance indeed? Shall we 57

---

28 Myrmidons followers of Achilles. **bottle-ale houses** (Used contemptuously of taverns because they sold low-class drink.) **33 testril** i.e.,
tester, a coin worth sixpence **35–36 good life** virtuous living. (Or perhaps Feste means simply "life's pleasures," but is misunderstood by
Sir Andrew to mean "virtuous living.") **51 sweet and twenty** i.e., sweet
and twenty times sweet **56 To . . . nose** i.e., to describe hearing in
olfactory terms. **dulcet in contagion** (Sir Toby may be mocking Sir
Andrew's unfortunate choice of words.) **57 make . . . dance** i.e., drink
till the sky seems to turn around

rouse the night owl in a catch that will draw three 58
souls out of one weaver? Shall we do that? 59

SIR ANDREW   An you love me, let's do 't. I am dog at a 60
catch. 61

FESTE   By 'r Lady, sir, and some dogs will catch well.

SIR ANDREW   Most certain. Let our catch be "Thou
knave."

FESTE   "Hold thy peace, thou knave," knight? I shall
be constrained in 't to call thee knave, knight.

SIR ANDREW   'Tis not the first time I have constrained
one to call me knave. Begin, Fool. It begins, "Hold thy
peace."

FESTE   I shall never begin if I hold my peace.

SIR ANDREW   Good, i' faith. Come, begin.   *Catch sung.*

Enter Maria.

MARIA   What a caterwauling do you keep here! If my
lady have not called up her steward Malvolio and bid
him turn you out of doors, never trust me.

SIR TOBY   My lady's a Cataian, we are politicians, Mal- 75
volio's a Peg-a-Ramsey, and [*Sings*] "Three merry 76
men be we." Am not I consanguineous? Am I not of 77
her blood? Tillyvally! Lady! [*Sings*.] "There dwelt a 78
man in Babylon, lady, lady." 79

FESTE   Beshrew me, the knight's in admirable fooling.

SIR ANDREW   Ay, he does well enough if he be disposed,
and so do I too. He does it with a better grace, but I
do it more natural. 83

SIR TOBY   [*Sings*]   "O' the twelfth day of December"— 84

58–59 draw three souls (Refers to the threefold nature of the soul,
vegetal, sensible, and intellectual; or to the three singers of the three-
part catch; or, just a comic exaggeration.)   **59 weaver** (Weavers were
often associated with psalm-singing.)   **60 dog at** very clever at. (But
Feste uses the word literally.)   **61 catch** round. (But Feste uses it to
mean "seize.")   **75 Cataian** Cathayan, i.e., Chinese, a trickster; or, just
nonsense.   **politicians** schemers, intriguers   **76 Peg-a-Ramsey** character
in a popular song. (Used here contemptuously.)   **76–77 Three . . . we** (A
snatch of an old song.)   **77 consanguineous** i.e., a blood relative of
Olivia   **78 Tillyvally** i.e., nonsense, fiddle-faddle   **78–79 There . . . lady**
(The first line of a ballad, "The Constancy of Susanna," together with
the refrain, "Lady, lady.")   **83 natural** naturally (but unconsciously
suggesting idiocy)   **84 O'. . . December** (Possibly part of a ballad about
the Battle of Musselburgh Field, or Toby's error for the "twelfth day of
Christmas," i.e., Twelfth Night.)

MARIA For the love o' God, peace!

   Enter Malvolio.

MALVOLIO My masters, are you mad? Or what are you?
Have you no wit, manners, nor honesty but to gabble
like tinkers at this time of night? Do ye make an alehouse of my lady's house that ye squeak out your coz-   89
iers' catches without any mitigation or remorse of   90
voice? Is there no respect of place, persons, nor time in
you?

SIR TOBY We did keep time, sir, in our catches. Sneck   93
up!   94

MALVOLIO Sir Toby, I must be round with you. My   95
lady bade me tell you that though she harbors you as
her kinsman, she's nothing allied to your disorders. If
you can separate yourself and your misdemeanors,
you are welcome to the house; if not, an it would
please you to take leave of her, she is very willing to
bid you farewell.

SIR TOBY [*Sings*]
  "Farewell, dear heart, since I must needs be gone."   102

MARIA Nay, good Sir Toby.

FESTE [*Sings*]
  "His eyes do show his days are almost done."

MALVOLIO Is 't even so?

SIR TOBY [*Sings*]
  "But I will never die."

FESTE
  Sir Toby, there you lie.

MALVOLIO This is much credit to you.

SIR TOBY [*Sings*]
  "Shall I bid him go?"

FESTE [*Sings*]
  "What an if you do?"

SIR TOBY [*Sings*]
  "Shall I bid him go, and spare not?"

FESTE [*Sings*]
  "O, no, no, no, no, you dare not."

89–90 coziers' cobblers' **90 mitigation or remorse** i.e., considerate
lowering **93–94 Sneck up** go hang **95 round** blunt **102 Farewell . . . gone** (From the ballad "Corydon's Farewell to Phyllis.")

SIR TOBY Out o' tune, sir? Ye lie. Art any more than a
steward? Dost thou think, because thou art virtuous,
there shall be no more cakes and ale?

FESTE Yes, by Saint Anne, and ginger shall be hot i' 116
the mouth too.

SIR TOBY Thou'rt i' the right. Go, sir, rub your chain 118
with crumbs. A stoup of wine, Maria! 119

MALVOLIO Mistress Mary, if you prized my lady's favor
at anything more than contempt, you would not give 121
means for this uncivil rule. She shall know of it, by 122
this hand.   *Exit.*

MARIA Go shake your ears. 124

SIR ANDREW 'Twere as good a deed as to drink when a
man's a-hungry, to challenge him the field, and then 126
to break promise with him and make a fool of him.

SIR TOBY Do 't, knight. I'll write thee a challenge, or I'll
deliver thy indignation to him by word of mouth.

MARIA Sweet Sir Toby, be patient for tonight. Since the
youth of the Count's was today with my lady, she is
much out of quiet. For Monsieur Malvolio, let me
alone with him. If I do not gull him into a nayword 133
and make him a common recreation, do not think I 134
have wit enough to lie straight in my bed. I know I
can do it.

SIR TOBY Possess us, possess us, tell us something of 137
him.

MARIA Marry, sir, sometimes he is a kind of puritan. 139

SIR ANDREW O, if I thought that, I'd beat him like a
dog.

SIR TOBY What, for being a puritan? Thy exquisite reason, dear knight?

---

116 Saint Anne mother of the Virgin Mary. (Her cult was derided in the
Reformation.) **ginger** (Commonly used to spice ale.) **118–119 Go . . .
crumbs** i.e., scour or polish your steward's chain; attend to your own
business and remember your station **121–122 give means** i.e., supply
drink **122 rule** conduct **124 your ears** i.e., your ass's ears **126 the
field** i.e., to a duel **133 gull** trick. **nayword** byword **134 recreation**
sport **137 Possess** inform **139 puritan** (Maria's point is that Malvolio
is sometimes a *kind* of puritan, insofar as he is precise about moral
conduct and censorious of others for immoral conduct, but that he is
nothing consistently except a time-server. He is not then simply a
satirical type of the Puritan sect. The extent of the resemblance is left
unstated.)

SIR ANDREW I have no exquisite reason for 't, but I have
reason good enough.

MARIA The devil a puritan that he is, or anything constantly, but a time-pleaser; an affectioned ass, that cons 147
state without book and utters it by great swaths; the 148
best persuaded of himself, so crammed, as he thinks, 149
with excellencies, that it is his grounds of faith that all 150
that look on him love him; and on that vice in him
will my revenge find notable cause to work.

SIR TOBY What wilt thou do?

MARIA I will drop in his way some obscure epistles of
love; wherein, by the color of his beard, the shape of
his leg, the manner of his gait, the expressure of his 156
eye, forehead, and complexion, he shall find himself 157
most feelingly personated. I can write very like my 158
lady your niece; on a forgotten matter we can hardly
make distinction of our hands.

SIR TOBY Excellent! I smell a device.

SIR ANDREW I have 't in my nose too.

SIR TOBY He shall think, by the letters that thou wilt
drop, that they come from my niece, and that she's in
love with him.

MARIA My purpose is indeed a horse of that color.

SIR ANDREW And your horse now would make him an
ass.

MARIA Ass, I doubt not.   169

SIR ANDREW O, 'twill be admirable!

MARIA Sport royal, I warrant you. I know my physic 171
will work with him. I will plant you two, and let the
Fool make a third, where he shall find the letter. Observe
his construction of it. For this night, to bed, and
dream on the event. Farewell.   *Exit.* 175

SIR TOBY Good night, Penthesilea.   176

---

147 time-pleaser time-server, sycophant. **afffectioned** affected
147–148 cons . . . book learns by heart the phrases and mannerisms of
the great **149 best persuaded** having the best opinion **150 grounds of
faith** creed, belief **156 expressure** expression **157 complexion** countenance **158 personated** represented **169 Ass, I** (with a pun on
"as I") **171 physic** medicine **175 event** outcome **176 Penthesilea**
Queen of the Amazons. (Another ironical allusion to Maria's diminutive
stature.)

SIR ANDREW   Before me, she's a good wench.   177

SIR TOBY   She's a beagle true-bred and one that adores me. What o' that?

SIR ANDREW   I was adored once too.

SIR TOBY   Let's to bed, knight. Thou hadst need send for more money.

SIR ANDREW   If I cannot recover your niece, I am a foul   183
way out.   184

SIR TOBY   Send for money, knight. If thou hast her not i' the end, call me cut.   186

SIR ANDREW   If I do not, never trust me, take it how you will.

SIR TOBY   Come, come, I'll go burn some sack. 'Tis too   189
late to go to bed now. Come, knight; come, knight.

                       Exeunt.

❖

2.4   *Enter Duke [Orsino], Viola, Curio,*
and others.

ORSINO
   Give me some music. Now, good morrow, friends.
   Now, good Cesario, but that piece of song,   2
   That old and antique song we heard last night;   3
   Methought it did relieve my passion much,
   More than light airs and recollected terms   5
   Of these most brisk and giddy-pacèd times.
   Come, but one verse.

CURIO   He is not here, so please your lordship, that should sing it.

ORSINO   Who was it?

CURIO   Feste the jester, my lord, a fool that the Lady Olivia's father took much delight in. He is about the house.

---

177 Before me i.e., on my soul   **183 recover** win   **183–184 foul way out**
i.e., miserably out of pocket. (Literally, out of my way and in the mire.)
186 cut a horse with a docked tail; also, a gelding, or the female genital
organ   **189 burn some sack** warm some Spanish wine

2.4. Location: Orsino's court.
2 but i.e., I ask only   **3 antique** old, quaint, fantastic   **5 recollected**
terms studied and artificial expressions (?)

ORSINO
　Seek him out, and play the tune the while.
　　　　　　　　　　　　[*Exit Curio.*] *Music plays.*
　Come hither, boy. If ever thou shalt love,
　In the sweet pangs of it remember me;
　For such as I am, all true lovers are,
　Unstaid and skittish in all motions else   18
　Save in the constant image of the creature
　That is beloved. How dost thou like this tune?

VIOLA
　It gives a very echo to the seat   21
　Where Love is throned.

ORSINO   Thou dost speak masterly.
　My life upon 't, young though thou art, thine eye
　Hath stayed upon some favor that it loves.   24
　Hath it not, boy?

VIOLA   A little, by your favor.   25

ORSINO
　What kind of woman is 't?

VIOLA   Of your complexion.

ORSINO
　She is not worth thee, then. What years, i' faith?

VIOLA　About your years, my lord.

ORSINO
　Too old, by heaven. Let still the woman take   29
　An elder than herself; so wears she to him,   30
　So sways she level in her husband's heart.   31
　For, boy, however we do praise ourselves,
　Our fancies are more giddy and unfirm,
　More longing, wavering, sooner lost and worn,
　Than women's are.

VIOLA   I think it well, my lord.

ORSINO
　Then let thy love be younger than thyself,
　Or thy affection cannot hold the bent;   37
　For women are as roses, whose fair flower
　Being once displayed, doth fall that very hour.

---

18 motions else other thoughts and emotions　**21 the seat** i.e., the heart
24 stayed . . . favor rested upon some face　**25 by your favor** (1) if you
please (2) like you in feature　**29 still** always　**30 wears she** she adapts
herself　**31 sways she level** she keeps steady, constant　**37 hold the bent**
hold steady (like the tension of a bow)

VIOLA

And so they are. Alas, that they are so,
To die, even when they to perfection grow!   41

Enter Curio and Clown [Feste].

ORSINO

O fellow, come, the song we had last night.
Mark it, Cesario, it is old and plain;
The spinsters and the knitters in the sun,   44
And the free maids that weave their thread with bones, 45
Do use to chant it. It is silly sooth,   46
And dallies with the innocence of love,
Like the old age.   48

FESTE   Are you ready, sir?

ORSINO   Ay, prithee, sing.   *Music.*

The Song.

FESTE

Come away, come away, death,
  And in sad cypress let me be laid.   52
Fly away, fly away, breath;
  I am slain by a fair cruel maid.
My shroud of white, stuck all with yew,   55
  O, prepare it!
My part of death, no one so true   57
  Did share it.   58

Not a flower, not a flower sweet
  On my black coffin let there be strown;   60
Not a friend, not a friend greet
  My poor corpse, where my bones shall be thrown.
A thousand thousand sighs to save,
  Lay me, O, where
Sad true lover never find my grave,
  To weep there!

---

41 even when just as   **44 spinsters** spinners   **45 free** carefree, innocent.
bones bobbins on which bone-lace was made   **46 Do use** are accustomed.
silly sooth simple truth   **48 Like . . . age** as in the good old times   **52 cypress** i.e., a coffin of cypress wood, or bier strewn with sprigs of cypress
55 yew i.e., yew sprigs. (Emblematic of mourning, like cypress.)   **57–58 My
. . . it** i.e., no one died for love so true to love as I   **60 strown** strewn

ORSINO There's for thy pains.   [*Offering money.*]
FESTE No pains, sir. I take pleasure in singing, sir.
ORSINO I'll pay thy pleasure then.
FESTE Truly, sir, and pleasure will be paid, one time 70
  or another.   71
ORSINO Give me now leave to leave thee.   72
FESTE Now, the melancholy god protect thee, and the   73
  tailor make thy doublet of changeable taffeta, for thy 74
  mind is a very opal. I would have men of such constancy put to sea, that their business might be every- 76
  thing and their intent everywhere, for that's it that 77
  always makes a good voyage of nothing. Farewell.   78
                                              Exit.

ORSINO
Let all the rest give place.
                    [*Curio and attendants withdraw.*]
                        Once more, Cesario,   79
Get thee to yond same sovereign cruelty.
Tell her my love, more noble than the world,
Prizes not quantity of dirty lands;
The parts that fortune hath bestowed upon her,   83
Tell her, I hold as giddily as fortune;   84
But 'tis that miracle and queen of gems   85
That nature pranks her in attracts my soul.   86
VIOLA But if she cannot love you, sir?
ORSINO
I cannot be so answered.
VIOLA   Sooth, but you must.
Say that some lady, as perhaps there is,

70–71 **pleasure . . . another** i.e., sooner or later one must pay for
indulgence 72 **leave to leave** permission to take leave of, dismiss
73 **the melancholy god** i.e., Saturn, whose planet was thought to control the melancholy temperament 74 **doublet** close-fitting jacket.
changeable taffeta a silk so woven of various-colored threads
that its color shifts with changing perspective 76–77 **that . . .
everywhere** i.e., so that in the changeableness of the sea their in-
constancy could always be exercised 77–78 **for . . . nothing** i.e., because such inconstant men would (1) make a good voyage come to
nothing but (2) think a voyage that led anywhere a good one 79 **give
place** withdraw 83 **parts** attributes such as wealth or rank 84 **I . . .
fortune** i.e., I esteem as carelessly as does fortune, that fickle goddess
85 **miracle . . . gems** i.e., her beauty 86 **pranks** adorns. **attracts** i.e.,
that attracts

Hath for your love as great a pang of heart
As you have for Olivia. You cannot love her;
You tell her so. Must she not then be answered?

ORSINO　There is no woman's sides
Can bide the beating of so strong a passion　　　94
As love doth give my heart; no woman's heart
So big, to hold so much; they lack retention.　　　96
Alas, their love may be called appetite,
No motion of the liver, but the palate,　　　98
That suffer surfeit, cloyment, and revolt;　　　99
But mine is all as hungry as the sea,
And can digest as much. Make no compare
Between that love a woman can bear me
And that I owe Olivia.

VIOLA　　　　　　　Ay, but I know—　　　103
ORSINO　What dost thou know?

VIOLA
Too well what love women to men may owe.
In faith, they are as true of heart as we.
My father had a daughter loved a man
As it might be perhaps, were I a woman,
I should your lordship.

ORSINO　　　　　　　And what's her history?

VIOLA
A blank, my lord. She never told her love,
But let concealment, like a worm i' the bud,
Feed on her damask cheek. She pined in thought,　　　112
And with a green and yellow melancholy
She sat like Patience on a monument,　　　114
Smiling at grief. Was not this love indeed?
We men may say more, swear more, but indeed
Our shows are more than will; for still we prove　　　117
Much in our vows, but little in our love.

ORSINO
But died thy sister of her love, my boy?

---

94 bide withstand　**96 retention** constancy, power of retaining
98 motion impulse.　**liver . . . palate** (Real love is a passion of the liver,
whereas fancy, light love, is born in the eye and nourished in the palate.)　**99 cloyment** satiety.　**revolt** sickness, revulsion　**103 owe** have
for　**112 damask** pink and white like the damask rose　**114 on a monument** carved in statuary on a tomb　**117 more than will** greater than
our feelings.　**still** always

VIOLA
I am all the daughters of my father's house,
And all the brothers too—and yet I know not.
Sir, shall I to this lady?
ORSINO   Ay, that's the theme.
To her in haste; give her this jewel. [*He gives a jewel.*] Say
My love can give no place, bide no denay.   *Exeunt.* 124

✢

2.5   *Enter Sir Toby, Sir Andrew, and Fabian.*

SIR TOBY   Come thy ways, Signor Fabian.
FABIAN   Nay, I'll come. If I lose a scruple of this sport, 2
let me be boiled to death with melancholy.   3
SIR TOBY   Wouldst thou not be glad to have the nig-
gardly rascally sheep-biter come by some notable 5
shame?
FABIAN   I would exult, man. You know he brought me
out o' favor with my lady about a bearbaiting here.
SIR TOBY   To anger him we'll have the bear again, and
we will fool him black and blue. Shall we not, Sir 10
Andrew?
SIR ANDREW   An we do not, it is pity of our lives.   12

        Enter Maria.

SIR TOBY   Here comes the little villain.—How now, my 13
metal of India?   14
MARIA   Get ye all three into the boxtree. Malvolio's
coming down this walk. He has been yonder i' the sun
practicing behavior to his own shadow this half hour.
Observe him, for the love of mockery, for I know this
letter will make a contemplative idiot of him. Close, in 19
the name of jesting! [*The others hide.*] Lie thou there

---

124 **can . . . denay** cannot yield or endure denial

2.5. Location: Olivia's garden.
2 **scruple** bit   3 **boiled** (with a pun on *biled;* black bile was the "humor"
of melancholy)   5 **sheep-biter** a dog that bites sheep, i.e., a nuisance
10 **fool . . . blue** mock him until he is figuratively black and blue
12 **pity of our lives** a pity we should live   13 **villain** (Here a term of
endearment.)   14 **metal** gold, i.e., priceless one   19 **contemplative** i.e.,
from his musings.   **Close** i.e., keep close, stay hidden

[*Throwing down a letter*]; for here comes the trout that
must be caught with tickling.   *Exit.* 22

     Enter Malvolio.

MALVOLIO   'Tis but fortune, all is fortune. Maria once
told me she did affect me; and I have heard herself 24
come thus near, that should she fancy, it should be 25
one of my complexion. Besides, she uses me with a
more exalted respect than anyone else that follows 27
her. What should I think on 't?

SIR TOBY   Here's an overweening rogue!

FABIAN   O, peace! Contemplation makes a rare turkey-
cock of him. How he jets under his advanced plumes! 31

SIR ANDREW   'Slight, I could so beat the rogue! 32

SIR TOBY   Peace, I say.

MALVOLIO   To be Count Malvolio.

SIR TOBY   Ah, rogue!

SIR ANDREW   Pistol him, pistol him.

SIR TOBY   Peace, peace!

MALVOLIO   There is example for 't. The lady of the Stra- 38
chy married the yeoman of the wardrobe. 39

SIR ANDREW   Fie on him, Jezebel! 40

FABIAN   O, peace! Now he's deeply in. Look how imagination blows him. 42

MALVOLIO   Having been three months married to her,
sitting in my state— 44

SIR TOBY   O, for a stone-bow, to hit him in the eye! 45

MALVOLIO   Calling my officers about me, in my
branched velvet gown; having come from a daybed, 47
where I have left Olivia sleeping—

SIR TOBY   Fire and brimstone!

FABIAN   O, peace, peace!

MALVOLIO   And then to have the humor of state; and 51

22 tickling (1) stroking gently about the gills—an actual method of
fishing (2) flattery   **24 she** i.e., Olivia.   **affect** have fondness for
25 fancy fall in love   **27 follows** serves   **31 jets** struts.   **advanced**
raised   **32 'Slight** by His (God's) light   **38 example** precedent
38–39 lady of the Strachy (Apparently a lady who had married below
her station; no certain identification.)   **40 Jezebel** the proud queen of
Ahab, King of Israel   **42 blows** puffs up   **44 state** chair of state
45 stone-bow crossbow that shoots stones   **47 branched** adorned with a
figured pattern suggesting branched leaves or flowers.   **daybed** sofa,
couch   **51 have . . . state** adopt the imperious manner of authority

after a demure travel of regard, telling them I know my 52
place as I would they should do theirs, to ask for my
kinsman Toby—   54

SIR TOBY   Bolts and shackles!

FABIAN   O, peace, peace, peace! Now, now.

MALVOLIO   Seven of my people, with an obedient start,
make out for him. I frown the while, and perchance
wind up my watch, or play with my—some rich 59
jewel. Toby approaches; curtsies there to me—

SIR TOBY   Shall this fellow live?

FABIAN   Though our silence be drawn from us with 62
cars, yet peace.   63

MALVOLIO   I extend my hand to him thus, quenching
my familiar smile with an austere regard of control— 65

SIR TOBY   And does not Toby take you a blow o' the lips 66
then?

MALVOLIO   Saying, "Cousin Toby, my fortunes having
cast me on your niece give me this prerogative of
speech—"

SIR TOBY   What, what?

MALVOLIO   "You must amend your drunkenness."

SIR TOBY   Out, scab!   73

FABIAN   Nay, patience, or we break the sinews of our
plot.

MALVOLIO   "Besides, you waste the treasure of your
time with a foolish knight—"

SIR ANDREW   That's me, I warrant you.

MALVOLIO   "One Sir Andrew—"

SIR ANDREW   I knew 'twas I, for many do call me fool.

MALVOLIO   What employment have we here?   81
                         [Taking up the letter.]

FABIAN   Now is the woodcock near the gin.   82

SIR TOBY   O, peace, and the spirit of humors intimate 83
reading aloud to him!

---

52 demure . . . regard grave survey of the company. **telling** indicating
to **54 Toby** (Malvolio omits the title *Sir*.) **59 play with my** (Malvolio
perhaps means his steward's chain, but checks himself in time; as
"Count Malvolio" he would not be wearing it. A bawdy meaning is also
suggested.) **62–63 with cars** with chariots, i.e., by force **65 familiar**
friendly. **regard of control** look of authority **66 take** deliver **73 scab**
scurvy fellow **81 employment** business **82 woodcock** (A bird proverbial for its stupidity.) **gin** snare **83 humors** whim, caprice

MALVOLIO By my life, this is my lady's hand. These be
her very c's, her u's, and her t's; and thus makes she 86
her great P's. It is in contempt of question her hand. 87
SIR ANDREW Her c's, her u's, and her t's. Why that?
MALVOLIO [*Reads*] "To the unknown beloved, this, and
my good wishes."—Her very phrases! By your leave, 90
wax. Soft! And the impressure her Lucrece, with 91
which she uses to seal. 'Tis my lady. To whom should 92
this be?   [*He opens the letter.*]
FABIAN This wins him, liver and all. 94
MALVOLIO [*Reads*]

> "Jove knows I love,
>   But who?
>   Lips, do not move;
>   No man must know."

"No man must know." What follows? The numbers 99
altered! "No man must know." If this should be thee,
Malvolio?
SIR TOBY Marry, hang thee, brock! 102
MALVOLIO [*Reads*]

> "I may command where I adore,
>   But silence, like a Lucrece knife,
>   With bloodless stroke my heart doth gore;
>   M.O.A.I. doth sway my life."

FABIAN A fustian riddle! 107
SIR TOBY Excellent wench, say I.
MALVOLIO "M.O.A.I. doth sway my life." Nay, but
first, let me see, let me see, let me see.
FABIAN What dish o' poison has she dressed him! 111
SIR TOBY And with what wing the staniel checks 112
at it! 113
MALVOLIO "I may command where I adore." Why, she
may command me; I serve her, she is my lady. Why,

---

86 c's . . . t's i.e., *cut*, slang for the female pudenda **87 great** (1) upper-
case (2) copious. **in contempt of** beyond **90–91 By . . . wax** (Addressed
to the seal on the letter.) **91 Soft** softly, not so fast. **impressure** device
imprinted on the seal. **Lucrece** Lucretia, chaste matron who, ravished
by Tarquin, committed suicide **92 uses** is accustomed **94 liver** i.e., the
seat of passion **99 numbers** meter **102 brock** badger. (Used contemptuously.) **107 fustian** bombastic, ridiculously pompous **111 dressed**
prepared for **112 staniel** kestrel, a sparrow hawk. (The word is used
contemptuously because of the uselessness of the staniel for fal-
conry.) **112–113 checks at it** turns to fly at it

this is evident to any formal capacity. There is no ob- 116
struction in this. And the end—what should that al-
phabetical position portend? If I could make that resemble something in me! Softly! M.O.A.I.—

SIR TOBY   O, ay, make up that. He is now at a cold scent. 120

FABIAN   Sowter will cry upon 't for all this, though it be 121
as rank as a fox.   122

MALVOLIO   M—Malvolio! M! Why, that begins my
name!

FABIAN   Did not I say he would work it out? The cur is
excellent at faults.   126

MALVOLIO   M—But then there is no consonancy in the 127
sequel that suffers under probation: A should follow, 128
but O does.

FABIAN   And O shall end, I hope.   130

SIR TOBY   Ay, or I'll cudgel him, and make him cry O!

MALVOLIO   And then I comes behind.

FABIAN   Ay, an you had any eye behind you, you might
see more detraction at your heels than fortunes before 134
you.

MALVOLIO   M.O.A.I. This simulation is not as the for- 136
mer. And yet, to crush this a little, it would bow to
me, for every one of these letters are in my name. Soft!
Here follows prose.

[*Reads.*] "If this fall into thy hand, revolve. In my stars 140
I am above thee, but be not afraid of greatness. Some
are born great, some achieve greatness, and some have
greatness thrust upon 'em. Thy Fates open their
hands; let thy blood and spirit embrace them; and, to
inure thyself to what thou art like to be, cast thy hum- 145

116 formal capacity normal mind   **120 O, ay** (playing on *O.I.* of
M.O.A.I.)   **make up** work out   **121 Sowter** cobbler. (Here, the name for
a hound.)   **cry upon 't** bay aloud (as though picking up the scent)
122 rank as a fox (i.e., Malvolio is so crude a hunter that he will leave
the trail of a hare and follow the rank scent of a fox.)   **126 at faults** i.e.,
at maneuvering his way past breaks in the line of scent   **127–128 consonancy in the sequel** pattern in the following letters. (In fact, the
letters M.O.A.I. represent the first, last, second, and next to last letters
of Malvolio's name.)   **128 suffers under probation** stands up under
examination   **130 O shall end** (1) O ends Malvolio's name (2) a noose
shall end his life (3) omega ends the Greek alphabet (4) his cry of pain
will end the joke   **134 detraction** defamation   **136 simulation** disguised
meaning   **140 revolve** consider.   **stars** fortune   **145 inure** accustom.
cast cast off

ble slough and appear fresh. Be opposite with a kins- 146
man, surly with servants. Let thy tongue tang argu- 147
ments of state; put thyself into the trick of singularity. 148
She thus advises thee that sighs for thee. Remember
who commended thy yellow stockings, and wished to
see thee ever cross-gartered. I say, remember. Go to, 151
thou art made, if thou desir'st to be so. If not, let me
see thee a steward still, the fellow of servants, and not
worthy to touch Fortune's fingers. Farewell. She that
would alter services with thee,   155
                    The Fortunate-Unhappy."
Daylight and champaign discovers not more! This is 157
open. I will be proud, I will read politic authors, I will 158
baffle Sir Toby, I will wash off gross acquaintance, I 159
will be point-devise the very man. I do not now fool 160
myself, to let imagination jade me; for every reason 161
excites to this, that my lady loves me. She did com-
mend my yellow stockings of late, she did praise my
leg being cross-gartered; and in this she manifests herself to my love, and with a kind of injunction drives
me to these habits of her liking. I thank my stars, I am 166
happy. I will be strange, stout, in yellow stockings, 167
and cross-gartered, even with the swiftness of putting
on. Jove and my stars be praised! Here is yet a post-
script. [*Reads.*] "Thou canst not choose but know who I
am. If thou entertain'st my love, let it appear in thy
smiling; thy smiles become thee well. Therefore in my
presence still smile, dear my sweet, I prithee." Jove, I
thank thee. I will smile; I will do everything that
thou wilt have me.   *Exit.*
FABIAN   I will not give my part of this sport for a pension of thousands to be paid from the Sophy.   177
SIR TOBY   I could marry this wench for this device.

---

146 slough skin of a snake; hence, former demeanor of humbleness.
opposite contradictory   **147 tang** sound loud with   **148 state** politics,
statecraft.   **trick of singularity** eccentricity of manner   **151 cross-gartered**
wearing garters above and below the knee so as to cross behind it
155 alter services i.e., exchange place of mistress and servant   **157 champaign** open country   **158 politic** dealing with state affairs   **159 baffle**
deride, degrade (a technical chivalric term used to describe the disgrace
of a perjured knight).   **gross** base   **160 point-devise** correct to the letter
161 jade trick   **166 these habits** this attire   **167 happy** fortunate.   **strange**
aloof.   **stout** haughty   **177 Sophy** Shah of Persia

SIR ANDREW   So could I too.

SIR TOBY   And ask no other dowry with her but such another jest.

Enter Maria.

SIR ANDREW   Nor I neither.

FABIAN   Here comes my noble gull-catcher.

SIR TOBY   Wilt thou set thy foot o' my neck?

SIR ANDREW   Or o' mine either?

SIR TOBY   Shall I play my freedom at tray-trip, and be- 186
come thy bondslave?

SIR ANDREW   I' faith, or I either?

SIR TOBY   Why, thou hast put him in such a dream that when the image of it leaves him he must run mad.

MARIA   Nay, but say true, does it work upon him?

SIR TOBY   Like aqua vitae with a midwife.   192

MARIA   If you will then see the fruits of the sport, mark his first approach before my lady. He will come to her in yellow stockings, and 'tis a color she abhors, and cross-gartered, a fashion she detests; and he will smile upon her, which will now be so unsuitable to her disposition, being addicted to a melancholy as she is, that it cannot but turn him into a notable contempt. If you 199 will see it, follow me.

SIR TOBY   To the gates of Tartar, thou most excellent 201 devil of wit!

SIR ANDREW   I'll make one too.   *Exeunt.*

❧

186 play gamble.   **tray-trip** a game of dice, success in which depended on throwing a three *(tray)*   **192 aqua vitae** brandy or other distilled liquors   **199 notable contempt** notorious object of contempt
201 Tartar Tartarus, the infernal regions

3.1 *Enter Viola, and Clown [Feste, playing his pipe and tabor].*

VIOLA Save thee, friend, and thy music. Dost thou live 1
by thy tabor? 2

FESTE No, sir, I live by the church.

VIOLA Art thou a churchman?

FESTE No such matter, sir. I do live by the church; for
I do live at my house, and my house doth stand by the
church.

VIOLA So thou mayst say the king lies by a beggar, if 8
a beggar dwell near him; or, the church stands by thy 9
tabor, if thy tabor stand by the church. 10

FESTE You have said, sir. To see this age! A sentence 11
is but a cheveril glove to a good wit. How quickly the 12
wrong side may be turned outward!

VIOLA Nay, that's certain. They that dally nicely with 14
words may quickly make them wanton. 15

FESTE I would therefore my sister had had no name,
sir.

VIOLA Why, man?

FESTE Why, sir, her name's a word, and to dally with
that word might make my sister wanton. But indeed, 20
words are very rascals since bonds disgraced them. 21

VIOLA Thy reason, man?

FESTE Troth, sir, I can yield you none without words,
and words are grown so false I am loath to prove reason with them.

VIOLA I warrant thou art a merry fellow and car'st for
nothing.

FESTE Not so, sir, I do care for something; but in my
conscience, sir, I do not care for you. If that be to care
for nothing, sir, I would it would make you invisible. 30

VIOLA Art not thou the Lady Olivia's fool?

3.1. Location: Olivia's garden.
1 Save God save **1–2 live by** earn your living with. (But Feste uses the
phrase to mean "dwell near.") **2 tabor** small drum **8 lies by** dwells
near **9–10 stands by . . . stand by** (1) is maintained by (2) is placed
near **11 sentence** maxim, judgment, opinion **12 cheveril** kidskin
14 dally nicely play subtly **15 wanton** i.e., unmanageable **20 wanton**
unchaste **21 since . . . them** i.e., since sworn statements have been
needed to make them good **30 invisible** i.e., nothing; absent

FESTE No indeed, sir, the Lady Olivia has no folly.
  She will keep no fool, sir, till she be married, and fools
  are as like husbands as pilchers are to herrings; the 34
  husband's the bigger. I am indeed not her fool, but
  her corrupter of words.

VIOLA I saw thee late at the Count Orsino's.   37

FESTE Foolery, sir, does walk about the orb like the 38
  sun; it shines everywhere. I would be sorry, sir, but 39
  the fool should be as oft with your master as with my
  mistress. I think I saw your wisdom there.   41

VIOLA Nay, an thou pass upon me, I'll no more with thee. 42
  Hold, there's expenses for thee.   [She gives a coin.]

FESTE Now Jove, in his next commodity of hair, send 44
  thee a beard!

VIOLA By my troth, I'll tell thee, I am almost sick for
  one—[Aside] though I would not have it grow on my
  chin.—Is thy lady within?

FESTE Would not a pair of these have bred, sir?

VIOLA Yes, being kept together and put to use.   50

FESTE I would play Lord Pandarus of Phrygia, sir, to 51
  bring a Cressida to this Troilus.

VIOLA I understand you, sir. 'Tis well begged.
                    [She gives another coin.]

FESTE The matter, I hope, is not great, sir, begging 54
  but a beggar; Cressida was a beggar. My lady is 55
  within, sir. I will conster to them whence you come. 56
  Who you are and what you would are out of my
  welkin—I might say "element," but the word is 58
  overworn.   Exit.

VIOLA
  This fellow is wise enough to play the fool,
  And to do that well craves a kind of wit.

34 pilchers pilchards, fish resembling herring **37 late** recently **38 orb**
earth **39 but** unless **41 your wisdom** i.e., you **42 pass upon me** fence
(verbally) with me, joke at my expense **44 commodity** supply **50 put
to use** put out at interest **51 Pandarus** the go-between in the love story
of Troilus and Cressida; uncle to Cressida **54–55 begging . . . Cressida**
(A reference to Henryson's *Testament of Cresseid* in which Cressida
became a leper and a beggar. Feste desires another coin to be the mate
of the one he has, as Cressida, the beggar, was mate to Troilus.)
56 conster construe, explain **58 welkin** sky. **element** (The word can be
synonymous with *welkin*, but the common phrase *out of my element*
means "beyond my scope.")

He must observe their mood on whom he jests,
The quality of persons, and the time,   63
And, like the haggard, check at every feather   64
That comes before his eye. This is a practice   65
As full of labor as a wise man's art;
For folly that he wisely shows is fit,   67
But wise men, folly-fall'n, quite taint their wit.   68

Enter Sir Toby and [Sir] Andrew.

SIR TOBY Save you, gentleman.
VIOLA And you, sir.
SIR ANDREW *Dieu vous garde, monsieur.*   71
VIOLA *Et vous aussi; votre serviteur.*   72
SIR ANDREW I hope, sir, you are, and I am yours.
SIR TOBY Will you encounter the house? My niece is   74
desirous you should enter, if your trade be to her.   75
VIOLA I am bound to your niece, sir; I mean she is the   76
list of my voyage.   77
SIR TOBY Taste your legs, sir, put them to motion.   78
VIOLA My legs do better understand me, sir, than I un-   79
derstand what you mean by bidding me taste my legs.
SIR TOBY I mean, to go, sir, to enter.
VIOLA I will answer you with gait and entrance.—But   82
we are prevented.   83

Enter Olivia and Gentlewoman [Maria].

Most excellent accomplished lady, the heavens rain
odors on you!
SIR ANDREW That youth's a rare courtier. "Rain odors,"
well.

---

63 quality character **64 haggard** untrained adult hawk, hence unmanageable **64–65 check . . . eye** strike at every bird it sees, i.e., dart
adroitly from subject to subject **65 practice** exercise of skill **67 folly
. . . fit** the folly he displays is a proper skill **68 folly-fall'n** having fallen
into folly. **taint** impair **71 Dieu . . . monsieur** God keep you, sir
72 Et . . . serviteur and you, too; (I am) your servant. (Sir Andrew is
not quite up to a reply in French.) **74 encounter** (High-sounding word
to express "enter.") **75 trade** course, path. (Viola picks up the commer-
cial meaning of the word in her reply.) **76 I am bound** I am on a
journey. (Continues Sir Toby's metaphor in *trade*.) **77 list** limit, destina-
tion **78 Taste** try **79 understand** stand under, support **82 gait and
entrance** going and entering **83 prevented** anticipated

VIOLA　My matter hath no voice, lady, but to your own　88
　most pregnant and vouchsafed ear.　89
SIR ANDREW　"Odors," "pregnant," and "vouchsafed."
　I'll get 'em all three all ready.　91
OLIVIA　Let the garden door be shut, and leave me to
　my hearing. [*Exeunt Sir Toby, Sir Andrew, and Maria.*]
　Give me your hand, sir.
VIOLA
　My duty, madam, and most humble service.
OLIVIA　What is your name?
VIOLA
　Cesario is your servant's name, fair princess.
OLIVIA
　My servant, sir? 'Twas never merry world
　Since lowly feigning was called compliment.　99
　You're servant to the Count Orsino, youth.
VIOLA
　And he is yours, and his must needs be yours;
　Your servant's servant is your servant, madam.
OLIVIA
　For him, I think not on him. For his thoughts,　103
　Would they were blanks, rather than filled with me!　104
VIOLA
　Madam, I come to whet your gentle thoughts
　On his behalf.
OLIVIA　　　　　　O, by your leave, I pray you.
　I bade you never speak again of him.
　But, would you undertake another suit,
　I had rather hear you to solicit that
　Than music from the spheres.
VIOLA　　　　　　　　　　Dear lady—　110
OLIVIA
　Give me leave, beseech you. I did send,
　After the last enchantment you did here,

88 hath no voice cannot be uttered　**89 pregnant** receptive.　**vouchsafed**
proffered, i.e., attentive　**91 all ready** i.e., for future use　**99 lowly
feigning** affected humility.　**was called** began to be called　**103 For** as
for　**104 blanks** blank spaces or empty sheets of paper　**110 music
from the spheres** (The heavenly bodies were thought to be fixed in
hollow concentric spheres that revolved one about the other, producing
a harmony too exquisite to be heard by human ears.)

A ring in chase of you; so did I abuse
Myself, my servant, and, I fear me, you.
Under your hard construction must I sit,   115
To force that on you in a shameful cunning   116
Which you knew none of yours. What might you think?
Have you not set mine honor at the stake   118
And baited it with all th' unmuzzled thoughts   119
That tyrannous heart can think? To one of your
      receiving   120
Enough is shown; a cypress, not a bosom,   121
Hides my heart. So, let me hear you speak.

VIOLA
  I pity you.

OLIVIA   That's a degree to love.

VIOLA
  No, not a grece; for 'tis a vulgar proof   124
  That very oft we pity enemies.

OLIVIA
  Why then methinks 'tis time to smile again.   126
  O world, how apt the poor are to be proud!   127
  If one should be a prey, how much the better
  To fall before the lion than the wolf!   *Clock strikes.* 129
  The clock upbraids me with the waste of time.
  Be not afraid, good youth, I will not have you;
  And yet, when wit and youth is come to harvest,
  Your wife is like to reap a proper man.   133
  There lies your way, due west.

VIOLA   Then westward ho!   134
  Grace and good disposition attend your ladyship.
  You'll nothing, madam, to my lord by me?

OLIVIA   Stay.
  I prithee, tell me what thou think'st of me.

---

115 hard construction harsh interpretation   **116 To force** for forcing
118 stake (The figure is from bearbaiting.)   **119 baited** harassed (as
dogs *bait* a bear)   **120 tyrannous** cruel.   **receiving** capacity, intelligence   **121 cypress** a thin, gauzelike, black material   **124 grece** step.
(Synonymous with *degree* in the preceding line.)   **vulgar proof** common
experience   **126 smile** i.e., cast off love's melancholy   **127 the poor** i.e.,
the unfortunate and rejected (like Olivia).   **proud** i.e., of their distress
129 To fall . . . wolf i.e., to fall before a noble adversary   **133 proper**
handsome, worthy   **134 westward ho** (The cry of Thames watermen to
attract westward-bound passengers from London to Westminster.)

VIOLA
That you do think you are not what you are.   139

OLIVIA
If I think so, I think the same of you.   140

VIOLA
Then think you right. I am not what I am.

OLIVIA
I would you were as I would have you be!

VIOLA
Would it be better, madam, than I am?
I wish it might, for now I am your fool.   144

OLIVIA
O, what a deal of scorn looks beautiful
In the contempt and anger of his lip!
A murderous guilt shows not itself more soon
Than love that would seem hid; love's night is noon.   148
Cesario, by the roses of the spring,
By maidhood, honor, truth, and everything,
I love thee so that, maugre all thy pride,   151
Nor wit nor reason can my passion hide.   152
Do not extort thy reasons from this clause,   153
For that I woo, thou therefore hast no cause;   154
But rather reason thus with reason fetter,   155
Love sought is good, but given unsought is better.

VIOLA
By innocence I swear, and by my youth,
I have one heart, one bosom, and one truth,
And that no woman has, nor never none
Shall mistress be of it save I alone.
And so adieu, good madam. Nevermore
Will I my master's tears to you deplore.   162

139 That . . . are i.e., that you think you are in love with a man, and you
are mistaken   **140 If . . . you** (Olivia may interpret Viola's cryptic
statement as suggesting that Olivia "does not know herself," i.e., is
distracted with passion; she may also hint at her suspicion that "Cesario" is higher born than he admits.)   **144 fool** butt   **148 love's . . . noon**
i.e., love, despite its attempt to be secret, reveals itself as plain as day
151 maugre in spite of   **152 Nor** neither   **153–154 Do . . . cause** i.e., do
not rationalize your indifference along these lines, that because I am the
wooer you have no cause to reciprocate   **155 But . . . fetter** but instead
take possession of your reasoning with the following reason   **162 deplore**
beweep

OLIVIA
Yet come again; for thou perhaps mayst move
That heart, which now abhors, to like his love.

                Exeunt [separately].

❖

3.2   *Enter Sir Toby, Sir Andrew, and Fabian.*

SIR ANDREW No, faith, I'll not stay a jot longer.
SIR TOBY Thy reason, dear venom, give thy reason.   2
FABIAN You must needs yield your reason, Sir Andrew.
SIR ANDREW Marry, I saw your niece do more favors to
  the Count's servingman than ever she bestowed upon
  me. I saw 't i' the orchard.   6
SIR TOBY Did she see thee the while, old boy? Tell me
  that.
SIR ANDREW As plain as I see you now.
FABIAN This was a great argument of love in her toward 10
  you.
SIR ANDREW 'Slight, will you make an ass o' me?   12
FABIAN I will prove it legitimate, sir, upon the oaths of 13
  judgment and reason.
SIR TOBY And they have been grand-jurymen since before Noah was a sailor.
FABIAN She did show favor to the youth in your sight
  only to exasperate you, to awake your dormouse valor, 18
  to put fire in your heart and brimstone in your liver.
  You should then have accosted her, and with some
  excellent jests, fire-new from the mint, you should
  have banged the youth into dumbness. This was 22
  looked for at your hand, and this was balked. The dou- 23
  ble gilt of this opportunity you let time wash off, and 24
  you are now sailed into the north of my lady's opinion, 25

3.2. Location: Olivia's house.
2 venom i.e., person filled with venom **6 orchard** garden **10 argu-ment** proof **12 'Slight** by his (God's) light **13 oaths** i.e., testimony under oath **18 dormouse** i.e., sleepy **22 banged** struck **23 balked** missed, neglected **23–24 double gilt** thick layer of gold, i.e., rare worth **25 north** i.e., out of the warmth and sunshine of her favor

where you will hang like an icicle on a Dutchman's ²⁶
beard, unless you do redeem it by some laudable at- ²⁷
tempt either of valor or policy.   ²⁸

SIR ANDREW An 't be any way, it must be with valor,
for policy I hate. I had as lief be a Brownist as a poli- ³⁰
tician.   ³¹

SIR TOBY Why, then, build me thy fortunes upon the ³²
basis of valor. Challenge me the Count's youth to fight
with him; hurt him in eleven places. My niece shall
take note of it; and assure thyself, there is no love-bro- ³⁵
ker in the world can more prevail in man's commen- ³⁶
dation with woman than report of valor.

FABIAN There is no way but this, Sir Andrew.

SIR ANDREW Will either of you bear me a challenge to
him?

SIR TOBY Go, write it in a martial hand. Be curst and ⁴¹
brief; it is no matter how witty, so it be eloquent and
full of invention. Taunt him with the license of ink. If ⁴³
thou "thou"-est him some thrice, it shall not be amiss; ⁴⁴
and as many lies as will lie in thy sheet of paper, al- ⁴⁵
though the sheet were big enough for the bed of Ware ⁴⁶
in England, set 'em down. Go, about it. Let there be
gall enough in thy ink, though thou write with a ⁴⁸
goose pen, no matter. About it.   ⁴⁹

SIR ANDREW Where shall I find you?

SIR TOBY We'll call thee at the cubiculo. Go.   ⁵¹

Exit Sir Andrew.

FABIAN This is a dear manikin to you, Sir Toby.   ⁵²

SIR TOBY I have been dear to him, lad, some two thou- ⁵³
sand strong, or so.

26–27 icicle . . . beard (Alludes to the arctic voyage of William Barentz
in 1596–1597.) **28 policy** stratagem **30 Brownist** (Early name of the
Congregationalists, from the name of the founder, Robert Browne.)
30–31 politician intriguer **32 build me** i.e., build **35–36 love-broker**
agent between lovers **41 curst** fierce **43 with . . . ink** i.e., with the
freedom that may be risked in writing but not in conversation
44 "thou"-est ("Thou" was used only between friends or to inferiors.)
45 lies charges of lying **46 bed of Ware** (A famous bedstead capable of
holding twelve persons, about eleven feet square, said to have been at
the Stag Inn in Ware, Hertfordshire.) **48 gall** (1) bitterness, rancor (2) a
growth found on certain oaks, used as an ingredient of ink **49 goose
pen** (1) goose quill (2) foolish style **51 call thee** call for you. **cubiculo**
little chamber **52 manikin** puppet **53 dear** expensive (playing on *dear*,
fond, in the previous speech)

FABIAN We shall have a rare letter from him; but you'll
not deliver 't?

SIR TOBY Never trust me, then; and by all means stir on
the youth to an answer. I think oxen and wainropes 58
cannot hale them together. For Andrew, if he were 59
opened and you find so much blood in his liver as will 60
clog the foot of a flea, I'll eat the rest of th' anatomy. 61

FABIAN And his opposite, the youth, bears in his vis- 62
age no great presage of cruelty.

Enter Maria.

SIR TOBY Look where the youngest wren of nine 64
comes.

MARIA If you desire the spleen, and will laugh your- 66
selves into stitches, follow me. Yond gull Malvolio is
turned heathen, a very renegado; for there is no Chris- 68
tian that means to be saved by believing rightly can
ever believe such impossible passages of grossness. 70
He's in yellow stockings.

SIR TOBY And cross-gartered?

MARIA Most villainously; like a pedant that keeps a 73
school i' the church. I have dogged him like his mur-
derer. He does obey every point of the letter that I
dropped to betray him. He does smile his face into
more lines than is in the new map with the augmen- 77
tation of the Indies. You have not seen such a thing as
'tis. I can hardly forbear hurling things at him. I know
my lady will strike him. If she do, he'll smile and
take 't for a great favor.

SIR TOBY Come, bring us, bring us where he is.

Exeunt omnes.

❖

58 wainropes wagon ropes   **59 hale** haul   **60 liver** (Seat of the passions.)   **61 anatomy** cadaver   **62 opposite** adversary   **64 youngest . . .
nine** i.e., the last hatched and smallest of a nest of wrens   **66 the spleen**
a laughing fit. (The spleen was thought to be the seat of immoderate
laughter.)   **68 renegado** renegade, deserter of his religion   **70 passages
of grossness** improbable statements (i.e., in the letter)   **73 villainously**
i.e., abominably.   **pedant** schoolmaster   **77 new map** (Probably a
reference to a map made by Emmeric Mollineux in 1599 for the pur-
chasers of Hakluyt's *Voyages*, showing more of the East Indies, including Japan, than had ever been mapped before.)

3.3   *Enter Sebastian and Antonio.*

SEBASTIAN
   I would not by my will have troubled you,
   But since you make your pleasure of your pains,
   I will no further chide you.
ANTONIO
   I could not stay behind you. My desire,
   More sharp than filèd steel, did spur me forth;
   And not all love to see you, though so much   6
   As might have drawn one to a longer voyage,
   But jealousy what might befall your travel,   8
   Being skilless in these parts, which to a stranger,   9
   Unguided and unfriended, often prove
   Rough and unhospitable. My willing love,
   The rather by these arguments of fear,   12
   Set forth in your pursuit.
SEBASTIAN   My kind Antonio,
   I can no other answer make but thanks,
   And thanks; and ever oft good turns   15
   Are shuffled off with such uncurrent pay.   16
   But were my worth, as is my conscience, firm,   17
   You should find better dealing. What's to do?   18
   Shall we go see the relics of this town?   19
ANTONIO
   Tomorrow, sir. Best first go see your lodging.
SEBASTIAN
   I am not weary, and 'tis long to night.
   I pray you, let us satisfy our eyes
   With the memorials and the things of fame
   That do renown this city.
ANTONIO   Would you'd pardon me.   24
   I do not without danger walk these streets.
   Once in a sea fight 'gainst the Count his galleys   26

3.3. Location: A street.
6 not all not only, not altogether   **8 jealousy** anxiety   **9 skilless in**
unacquainted with   **12 The rather** the more quickly   **15 And . . . turns**
(This probably corrupt line is usually made to read, "And thanks and
ever thanks; and oft good turns.")   **16 uncurrent** worthless (such as
mere thanks)   **17 worth** wealth.   **conscience** i.e., moral inclination to
assist   **18 dealing** treatment   **19 relics** antiquities   **24 renown** make
famous   **26 Count his** Count's, i.e., Duke's

I did some service, of such note indeed
That were I ta'en here it would scarce be answered.   28

SEBASTIAN
Belike you slew great number of his people?   29

ANTONIO
Th' offense is not of such a bloody nature,
Albeit the quality of the time and quarrel
Might well have given us bloody argument.   32
It might have since been answered in repaying   33
What we took from them, which for traffic's sake   34
Most of our city did. Only myself stood out,
For which, if I be lapsèd in this place,   36
I shall pay dear.

SEBASTIAN   Do not then walk too open.

ANTONIO
It doth not fit me. Hold, sir, here's my purse.
                [*He gives his purse.*]
In the south suburbs, at the Elephant,   39
Is best to lodge. I will bespeak our diet,   40
Whiles you beguile the time and feed your knowledge
With viewing of the town. There shall you have me.

SEBASTIAN   Why I your purse?

ANTONIO
Haply your eye shall light upon some toy   44
You have desire to purchase; and your store   45
I think is not for idle markets, sir.   46

SEBASTIAN
I'll be your purse-bearer and leave you
For an hour.

ANTONIO   To th' Elephant.

SEBASTIAN   I do remember.
                     Exeunt [*separately*].

❧

---

28 it . . . answered i.e., I'd be hard put to offer a defense   **29 Belike** probably, perhaps   **32 bloody argument** cause for bloodshed   **33 answered** compensated   **34 traffic's** trade's   **36 lapsèd** i.e., caught   **39 Elephant** (The name of an inn.)   **40 bespeak our diet** order our food   **44 toy** trifle   **45 store** store of money   **46 idle markets** unnecessary purchases, luxuries

3.4 *Enter Olivia and Maria.*

OLIVIA *[Aside]*
  I have sent after him; he says he'll come. 1
  How shall I feast him? What bestow of him? 2
  For youth is bought more oft than begged or borrowed.
  I speak too loud.—
  Where's Malvolio? He is sad and civil, 5
  And suits well for a servant with my fortunes.
  Where is Malvolio?
MARIA He's coming, madam, but in very strange man-
  ner. He is, sure, possessed, madam. 9
OLIVIA Why, what's the matter? Does he rave?
MARIA No, madam, he does nothing but smile. Your
  ladyship were best to have some guard about you if
  he come, for sure the man is tainted in 's wits.
OLIVIA
  Go call him hither. *[Maria summons Malvolio.]* I am as
    mad as he,
  If sad and merry madness equal be.

    Enter Malvolio.

  How now, Malvolio?
MALVOLIO Sweet lady, ho, ho!
OLIVIA Smil'st thou? I sent for thee upon a sad occasion.
MALVOLIO Sad, lady? I could be sad. This does make
  some obstruction in the blood, this cross-gartering,
  but what of that? If it please the eye of one, it is with
  me as the very true sonnet is, "Please one and please 23
  all." 24
OLIVIA Why, how dost thou, man? What is the matter
  with thee?
MALVOLIO Not black in my mind, though yellow in my 27
  legs. It did come to his hands, and commands shall be 28
  executed. I think we do know the sweet Roman hand. 29

3.4. Location: Olivia's garden.
1 he . . . come i.e., suppose he says he'll come 2 of on 5 sad and civil
sober and decorous 9 possessed i.e., possessed with an evil spirit
23 sonnet song, ballad 23–24 Please . . . all (The refrain of a ballad.)
27 black i.e., melancholic 28 It i.e., the letter 29 Roman hand fash-
ionable Italian style of handwriting

OLIVIA   Wilt thou go to bed, Malvolio?

MALVOLIO   To bed? Ay, sweetheart, and I'll come to 31
thee.   32

OLIVIA   God comfort thee! Why dost thou smile so and
kiss thy hand so oft?

MARIA   How do you, Malvolio?

MALVOLIO   At your request? Yes, nightingales answer 36
daws.   37

MARIA   Why appear you with this ridiculous boldness
before my lady?

MALVOLIO   "Be not afraid of greatness." 'Twas well writ.

OLIVIA   What mean'st thou by that, Malvolio?

MALVOLIO   "Some are born great—"

OLIVIA   Ha?

MALVOLIO   "Some achieve greatness—"

OLIVIA   What sayst thou?

MALVOLIO   "And some have greatness thrust upon
them."

OLIVIA   Heaven restore thee!

MALVOLIO   "Remember who commended thy yellow
stockings—"

OLIVIA   Thy yellow stockings?

MALVOLIO   "And wished to see thee cross-gartered."

OLIVIA   Cross-gartered?

MALVOLIO   "Go to, thou art made, if thou desir'st to
be so—"

OLIVIA   Am I made?

MALVOLIO   "If not, let me see thee a servant still."

OLIVIA   Why, this is very midsummer madness.   58

     Enter Servant.

SERVANT   Madam, the young gentleman of the Count
Orsino's is returned. I could hardly entreat him back.
He attends your ladyship's pleasure.

OLIVIA   I'll come to him. [*Exit Servant.*] Good Maria, let
this fellow be looked to. Where's my cousin Toby? Let
some of my people have a special care of him. I would

31–32 **Ay . . . thee** (Malvolio quotes from a popular song of the day.)
36–37 **nightingales answer daws** i.e., (to Maria), do you suppose a fine
fellow like me would answer a lowly creature (a *daw*, a crow) like you
58 **midsummer madness** (A proverbial phrase; the midsummer moon
was supposed to cause madness.)

not have him miscarry for the half of my dowry.   65

    Exeunt [Olivia and Maria, different ways.]

MALVOLIO O ho, do you come near me now? No worse 66
man than Sir Toby to look to me! This concurs directly
with the letter. She sends him on purpose that I may
appear stubborn to him, for she incites me to that in
the letter. "Cast thy humble slough," says she; "be opposite with a kinsman, surly with servants; let thy
tongue tang with arguments of state; put thyself into
the trick of singularity." And consequently sets down 73
the manner how: as, a sad face, a reverend carriage, a 74
slow tongue, in the habit of some sir of note, and so 75
forth. I have limed her, but it is Jove's doing, and Jove 76
make me thankful! And when she went away now,
"Let this fellow be looked to." "Fellow!" Not "Malvo- 78
lio," nor after my degree, but "fellow." Why, every- 79
thing adheres together, that no dram of a scruple, no 80
scruple of a scruple, no obstacle, no incredulous or un- 81
safe circumstance—What can be said? Nothing that 82
can be can come between me and the full prospect of
my hopes. Well, Jove, not I, is the doer of this, and he
is to be thanked.

    Enter [Sir] Toby, Fabian, and Maria.

SIR TOBY Which way is he, in the name of sanctity? If
all the devils of hell be drawn in little, and Legion him- 87
self possessed him, yet I'll speak to him.

FABIAN Here he is, here he is.—How is 't with you, sir?
How is 't with you, man?

MALVOLIO Go off. I discard you. Let me enjoy my pri- 91
vate. Go off.   92

MARIA Lo, how hollow the fiend speaks within him!

---

65 miscarry come to harm **66 come near** understand **73 consequently**
thereafter **74 sad** serious **75 habit . . . note** attire suited to a gentleman of distinction **76 limed** caught like a bird with birdlime (a sticky
substance spread on branches) **78 Fellow** (Malvolio takes the original
meaning, "companion.") **79 after my degree** according to my position **80 dram** (Literally, one-eighth of a fluid ounce.) **scruple** (Literally, one-third of a dram.) **81 incredulous** incredible **81–82 unsafe**
uncertain, unreliable **87 drawn in little** gathered into a small space,
i.e., in Malvolio's heart. **Legion** (Cf. "My name is Legion, for we are
many," Mark 5:9.) **91–92 private** privacy

Did not I tell you? Sir Toby, my lady prays you to have a care of him.

MALVOLIO Aha, does she so?

SIR TOBY Go to, go to! Peace, peace, we must deal gently with him. Let me alone.—How do you, Malvolio? How is 't with you? What, man, defy the devil! Consider, he's an enemy to mankind.

MALVOLIO Do you know what you say?

MARIA La you, an you speak ill of the devil, how he takes it at heart! Pray God he be not bewitched!

FABIAN Carry his water to the wisewoman.

MARIA Marry, and it shall be done tomorrow morning, if I live. My lady would not lose him for more than I'll say.

MALVOLIO How now, mistress?

MARIA O Lord!

SIR TOBY Prithee, hold thy peace; this is not the way. Do you not see you move him? Let me alone with him.

FABIAN No way but gentleness, gently, gently. The fiend is rough, and will not be roughly used.

SIR TOBY Why, how now, my bawcock? How dost thou, chuck?

MALVOLIO Sir!

SIR TOBY Ay, biddy, come with me. What, man, 'tis not for gravity to play at cherry-pit with Satan. Hang him, foul collier!

MARIA Get him to say his prayers, good Sir Toby, get him to pray.

MALVOLIO My prayers, minx?

MARIA No, I warrant you, he will not hear of godliness.

MALVOLIO Go hang yourselves all! You are idle shallow things; I am not of your element. You shall know more hereafter.   *Exit.*

SIR TOBY Is 't possible?

---

98 Let me alone leave him to me   **102 La you** look you   **104 water** urine (for medical analysis)   **115 bawcock** fine fellow. (From French *beau-coq*.)   **116 chuck** (A form of "chick," term of endearment.)   **118 biddy** chicken   **119 for gravity** suitable for a man of your dignity. **cherry-pit** a children's game consisting of throwing cherry stones into a hole   **120 collier** i.e., Satan. (Literally, a coal vendor.)   **126–127 know more** i.e., hear about this

FABIAN If this were played upon a stage now, I could
  condemn it as an improbable fiction.
SIR TOBY His very genius hath taken the infection of the 131
  device, man.
MARIA Nay, pursue him now, lest the device take air 133
  and taint.   134
FABIAN Why, we shall make him mad indeed.
MARIA The house will be the quieter.
SIR TOBY Come, we'll have him in a dark room and
  bound. My niece is already in the belief that he's mad.
  We may carry it thus, for our pleasure and his pen-
  ance, till our very pastime, tired out of breath, prompt
  us to have mercy on him; at which time we will bring
  the device to the bar and crown thee for a finder of 142
  madmen. But see, but see!

  Enter Sir Andrew [with a letter].

FABIAN More matter for a May morning.   144
SIR ANDREW Here's the challenge. Read it. I warrant
  there's vinegar and pepper in 't.
FABIAN Is 't so saucy?   147
SIR ANDREW Ay, is 't, I warrant him. Do but read.
SIR TOBY Give me. [*Reads.*] "Youth, whatsoever thou
  art, thou art but a scurvy fellow."
FABIAN Good, and valiant.
SIR TOBY [*Reads*] "Wonder not, nor admire not in thy 152
  mind, why I do call thee so, for I will show thee no
  reason for 't."
FABIAN A good note, that keeps you from the blow of 155
  the law.
SIR TOBY [*Reads*] "Thou com'st to the Lady Olivia, and
  in my sight she uses thee kindly. But thou liest in thy
  throat; that is not the matter I challenge thee for."
FABIAN Very brief, and to exceeding good sense—less.
SIR TOBY [*Reads*] "I will waylay thee going home,
  where if it be thy chance to kill me—"
FABIAN Good.

131 **genius** i.e., soul, spirit 133–134 **take . . . taint** become exposed to
air (i.e., become known) and thus spoil 142 **bar** i.e., bar of judgment
144 **matter . . . morning** sport for Mayday 147 **saucy** (1) spicy
(2) insolent 152 **admire** marvel 155 **note** observation, remark

SIR TOBY [*Reads*] "Thou kill'st me like a rogue and a villain."

FABIAN Still you keep o' the windy side of the law. 166 Good.

SIR TOBY [*Reads*] "Fare thee well, and God have mercy upon one of our souls! He may have mercy upon mine, but my hope is better, and so look to thyself. Thy friend, as thou usest him, and thy sworn enemy,
                                         Andrew Aguecheek."
If this letter move him not, his legs cannot. I'll give 't him.

MARIA You may have very fit occasion for 't. He is now in some commerce with my lady, and will by and by 176 depart.

SIR TOBY Go, Sir Andrew. Scout me for him at the cor- 178 ner of the orchard like a bum-baily. So soon as ever 179 thou seest him, draw, and as thou draw'st, swear hor-rible; for it comes to pass oft that a terrible oath, with a swaggering accent sharply twanged off, gives man-hood more approbation than ever proof itself would 183 have earned him. Away!

SIR ANDREW Nay, let me alone for swearing.   *Exit.* 185

SIR TOBY Now will not I deliver his letter; for the behav-ior of the young gentleman gives him out to be of good capacity and breeding; his employment between his lord and my niece confirms no less. Therefore this letter, being so excellently ignorant, will breed no ter-ror in the youth. He will find it comes from a clodpoll. 191 But, sir, I will deliver his challenge by word of mouth, set upon Aguecheek a notable report of valor, and drive the gentleman, as I know his youth will aptly receive it, into a most hideous opinion of his rage, skill, fury, and impetuosity. This will so fright them both that they will kill one another by the look, like cockatrices.   198

---

166 windy windward, i.e., safe, where the law may get no scent of you **176 commerce** conference **178 Scout me** keep watch **179 bum-baily** minor sheriff's officer employed in making arrests **183 approbation** reputation (for courage). **proof** performance **185 let . . . swearing** don't worry about my ability in swearing **191 clodpoll** blockhead **198 cockatrices** basilisks, fabulous serpents reputed to be able to kill by a mere look

Enter Olivia and Viola.

FABIAN   Here he comes with your niece. Give them way   199
till he take leave, and presently after him.   200
SIR TOBY   I will meditate the while upon some horrid   201
message for a challenge.
                    [*Exeunt Sir Toby, Fabian, and Maria.*]
OLIVIA
I have said too much unto a heart of stone
And laid mine honor too unchary on 't.   204
There's something in me that reproves my fault,
But such a headstrong potent fault it is
That it but mocks reproof.
VIOLA
With the same havior that your passion bears
Goes on my master's griefs.
OLIVIA [*Giving a locket*]
Here, wear this jewel for me. 'Tis my picture.   210
Refuse it not; it hath no tongue to vex you.
And I beseech you come again tomorrow.
What shall you ask of me that I'll deny,
That honor, saved, may upon asking give?   214
VIOLA
Nothing but this: your true love for my master.
OLIVIA
How with mine honor may I give him that
Which I have given to you?
VIOLA   I will acquit you.   217
OLIVIA
Well, come again tomorrow. Fare thee well.
A fiend like thee might bear my soul to hell.   [*Exit.*]   219

    Enter [Sir] Toby and Fabian.

SIR TOBY   Gentleman, God save thee.
VIOLA   And you, sir.
SIR TOBY   That defense thou hast, betake thee to 't. Of
what nature the wrongs are thou hast done him, I

---

199 Give them way stay out of their way   **200 presently** immediately
201 horrid terrifying (literally, "bristling")   **204 laid** hazarded.   **unchary on 't** recklessly on it   **210 jewel** (Any piece of jewelry; here,
seemingly, a locket.)   **214 That . . . give** i.e., that can be granted without
compromising any honor   **217 acquit you** release you of your promise
219 like resembling

know not; but thy intercepter, full of despite, bloody   224
as the hunter, attends thee at the orchard end. Dis-   225
mount thy tuck, be yare in thy preparation, for thy   226
assailant is quick, skillful, and deadly.

VIOLA You mistake sir. I am sure no man hath any
quarrel to me. My remembrance is very free and clear
from any image of offense done to any man.

SIR TOBY You'll find it otherwise, I assure you. Therefore, if you hold your life at any price, betake you to
your guard; for your opposite hath in him what youth,
strength, skill, and wrath can furnish man withal.

VIOLA I pray you, sir, what is he?

SIR TOBY He is knight, dubbed with unhatched rapier   236
and on carpet consideration, but he is a devil in   237
private brawl. Souls and bodies hath he divorced
three, and his incensement at this moment·is so im-
placable that satisfaction can be none but by pangs of
death and sepulcher. Hob, nob, is his word; give 't or   241
take 't.

VIOLA I will return again into the house and desire
some conduct of the lady. I am no fighter. I have heard   244
of some kind of men that put quarrels purposely on
others, to taste their valor. Belike this is a man of that   246
quirk.   247

SIR TOBY Sir, no. His indignation derives itself out of a
very competent injury; therefore, get you on and give   249
him his desire. Back you shall not to the house, unless
you undertake that with me which with as much   251
safety you might answer him. Therefore, on, or strip
your sword stark naked; for meddle you must, that's   253
certain, or forswear to wear iron about you.   254

VIOLA This is as uncivil as strange. I beseech you, do
me this courteous office, as to know of the knight what

---

224 intercepter i.e., he who lies in wait. **despite** defiance **224–225 bloody
as the hunter** bloodthirsty as a hunting dog **225–226 Dismount thy
tuck** draw your rapier **226 yare** ready, nimble **236 unhatched** un-
hacked, unused in battle **237 carpet consideration** (A carpet knight was
one whose title was obtained not in battle but through connections at
court.) **241 Hob, nob** have or have not, i.e., give it or take it. **word**
motto **244 conduct** escort **246 taste** test **247 quirk** peculiar humor
249 competent sufficient **251 that** i.e., to give satisfaction in a duel
253 meddle engage (in conflict) **254 forswear . . . iron** give up your
right to wear a sword

my offense to him is. It is something of my negligence,
nothing of my purpose.

SIR TOBY   I will do so. Signor Fabian, stay you by this
gentleman till my return.   *Exit Toby.*

VIOLA   Pray you, sir, do you know of this matter?

FABIAN   I know the knight is incensed against you, even
to a mortal arbitrament, but nothing of the circum-   263
stance more.

VIOLA   I beseech you, what manner of man is he?

FABIAN   Nothing of that wonderful promise, to read   266
him by his form, as you are like to find him in the   267
proof of his valor. He is, indeed, sir, the most skillful,
bloody, and fatal opposite that you could possibly
have found in any part of Illyria. Will you walk towards him? I will make your peace with him if I can.

VIOLA   I shall be much bound to you for 't. I am one that
had rather go with Sir Priest than Sir Knight. I care not   273
who knows so much of my mettle.   *Exeunt.*

Enter [Sir] Toby and [Sir] Andrew.

SIR TOBY   Why, man, he's a very devil; I have not seen
such a firago. I had a pass with him, rapier, scabbard,   276
and all, and he gives me the stuck in with such a mor-   277
tal motion that it is inevitable; and on the answer, he   278
pays you as surely as your feet hits the ground they
step on. They say he has been fencer to the Sophy.

SIR ANDREW   Pox on 't, I'll not meddle with him.

SIR TOBY   Ay, but he will not now be pacified. Fabian
can scarce hold him yonder.

SIR ANDREW   Plague on 't, an I thought he had been valiant and so cunning in fence, I'd have seen him
damned ere I'd have challenged him. Let him let the
matter slip, and I'll give him my horse, gray Capilet.   287

SIR TOBY   I'll make the motion. Stand here, make a good   288
show on 't. This shall end without the perdition of   289
souls. [*Aside, as he crosses to meet Fabian.*] Marry, I'll   290
ride your horse as well as I ride you.

---

263 **mortal arbitrament** trial to the death   266–267 **read . . . form** judge
him by his appearance   273 **Sir Priest** (*Sir* was a courtesy title for priests.)
276 **firago** virago.   **pass** bout   277 **stuck in** stoccado, a thrust in fencing   278 **answer** return hit   287 **Capilet** i.e., "little horse." (From "ca-
pel," a nag.)   288 **motion** offer   289–290 **perdition of souls** loss of lives

Enter Fabian and Viola.

[*To Fabian.*] I have his horse to take up the quarrel. I 292
have persuaded him the youth's a devil.

FABIAN   He is as horribly conceited of him, and pants 294
and looks pale as if a bear were at his heels.

SIR TOBY [*To Viola*]   There's no remedy, sir, he will fight
with you for 's oath's sake. Marry, he hath better be-
thought him of his quarrel, and he finds that now
scarce to be worth talking of. Therefore draw, for the
supportance of his vow; he protests he will not hurt 300
you.

VIOLA [*Aside*]   Pray God defend me! A little thing
would make me tell them how much I lack of a man.

FABIAN   Give ground, if you see him furious.

SIR TOBY [*Crossing to Sir Andrew*]   Come, Sir Andrew,
there's no remedy. The gentleman will, for his
honor's sake, have one bout with you. He cannot by
the *duello* avoid it. But he has promised me, as he is 308
a gentleman and a soldier, he will not hurt you. Come
on, to 't.

SIR ANDREW   Pray God he keep his oath!

VIOLA   I do assure you, 'tis against my will.

[*They draw.*]

Enter Antonio.

ANTONIO
Put up your sword. If this young gentleman
Have done offense, I take the fault on me;
If you offend him, I for him defy you.

SIR TOBY   You, sir? Why, what are you?

ANTONIO
One, sir, that for his love dares yet do more
Than you have heard him brag to you he will.

SIR TOBY
Nay, if you be an undertaker, I am for you. 319

[*They draw.*]

Enter Officers.

292 take up settle, make up   **294 He . . . him** i.e., Cesario has as
horrible a conception of Sir Andrew   **300 supportance** upholding
308 duello duelling code   **319 undertaker** one who takes upon himself a
task or business; here, a challenger.   **for you** i.e., ready for you

FABIAN O good Sir Toby, hold! Here come the officers.

SIR TOBY [*To Antonio*] I'll be with you anon.

VIOLA [*To Sir Andrew*] Pray, sir, put your sword up, if
you please.

SIR ANDREW Marry, will I, sir; and for that I promised
you, I'll be as good as my word. He will bear you eas- 325
ily, and reins well.

FIRST OFFICER This is the man; do thy office.

SECOND OFFICER
    Antonio, I arrest thee at the suit
    Of Count Orsino.

ANTONIO   You do mistake me, sir.

FIRST OFFICER
    No, sir, no jot. I know your favor well,   330
    Though now you have no sea-cap on your head.—
    Take him away. He knows I know him well.

ANTONIO
    I must obey. [*To Viola.*] This comes with seeking you.
    But there's no remedy, I shall answer it.   334
    What will you do, now my necessity
    Makes me to ask you for my purse? It grieves me
    Much more for what I cannot do for you
    Than what befalls myself. You stand amazed,
    But be of comfort.

SECOND OFFICER   Come, sir, away.

ANTONIO
    I must entreat of you some of that money.

VIOLA What money, sir?
    For the fair kindness you have showed me here,
    And part being prompted by your present trouble,   343
    Out of my lean and low ability
    I'll lend you something. My having is not much;   345
    I'll make division of my present with you.   346
    Hold, there's half my coffer.   [*She offers money.*]   347

ANTONIO Will you deny me now?
    Is 't possible that my deserts to you   349
    Can lack persuasion? Do not tempt my misery,   350
    Lest that it make me so unsound a man   351

---

325 He i.e., the horse **330 favor** face **334 answer it** suffer for it **343 part**
partly **345 having** wealth **346 present** present store **347 coffer** purse.
(Literally, strong box.) **349–350 deserts . . . persuasion** claims on you
can fail to persuade you to help me **351 unsound** weak

As to upbraid you with those kindnesses
That I have done for you.

VIOLA   I know of none,
Nor know I you by voice or any feature.
I hate ingratitude more in a man
Than lying, vainness, babbling drunkenness,
Or any taint of vice whose strong corruption
Inhabits our frail blood.

ANTONIO   O heavens themselves!

SECOND OFFICER   Come, sir, I pray you, go.

ANTONIO
Let me speak a little. This youth that you see here
I snatched one half out of the jaws of death,
Relieved him with such sanctity of love,
And to his image, which methought did promise   364
Most venerable worth, did I devotion.   365

FIRST OFFICER
What's that to us? The time goes by. Away!

ANTONIO
But, O, how vile an idol proves this god!
Thou hast, Sebastian, done good feature shame.   368
In nature there's no blemish but the mind;
None can be called deformed but the unkind.   370
Virtue is beauty, but the beauteous evil   371
Are empty trunks o'erflourished by the devil.   372

FIRST OFFICER
The man grows mad. Away with him! Come, come, sir.

ANTONIO   Lead me on.   *Exit [with Officers]*.

VIOLA [*To herself*]
Methinks his words do from such passion fly
That he believes himself; so do not I.   376
Prove true, imagination, O, prove true,
That I, dear brother, be now ta'en for you!

SIR TOBY   Come hither, knight; come hither, Fabian.

364 image what he appeared to be (playing on the idea of a religious
icon to be venerated)   **365 venerable worth** worthiness of being venerated   **368 Thou . . . shame** i.e., you have shamed physical beauty by
showing that it does not always reflect inner beauty   **370 unkind**
unnatural   **371 beauteous evil** those who are outwardly beautiful but
evil within   **372 trunks** (1) chests (2) bodies.   **o'erflourished** (1) cov-
ered with ornamental carvings (2) made outwardly beautiful   **376 so**
. . . I i.e., I do not believe myself (in the hope that has arisen in me)

We'll whisper o'er a couplet or two of most sage saws. 380
[*They gather apart from Viola.*]

VIOLA
He named Sebastian. I my brother know   381
Yet living in my glass; even such and so   382
In favor was my brother, and he went
Still in this fashion, color, ornament,
For him I imitate. O, if it prove,   385
Tempests are kind, and salt waves fresh in love!

[*Exit.*]

SIR TOBY   A very dishonest, paltry boy, and more a cow- 387
ard than a hare. His dishonesty appears in leaving his 388
friend here in necessity and denying him; and for his 389
cowardship, ask Fabian.

FABIAN   A coward, a most devout coward, religious in it.

SIR ANDREW   'Slid, I'll after him again and beat him.   392

SIR TOBY   Do, cuff him soundly, but never draw thy
sword.

SIR ANDREW   An I do not—   [*Exit.*]

FABIAN   Come, let's see the event.   396

SIR TOBY   I dare lay any money 'twill be nothing yet.   397

Exeunt.

❧

380 saws sayings   **381–382 I . . . glass** i.e., I know my brother is virtu-
ally alive every time I look in a mirror, because we looked so much
alike   **385 prove** prove true   **387 dishonest** dishonorable   **388 dishonesty** dishonor   **389 denying** refusing to acknowledge   **392 'Slid** i.e., by
his (God's) eyelid   **396 event** outcome   **397 yet** nevertheless, after all

4.1   *Enter Sebastian and Clown [Feste].*

FESTE Will you make me believe that I am not sent for
you?

SEBASTIAN Go to, go to, thou art a foolish fellow. Let
me be clear of thee.

FESTE Well held out, i' faith! No, I do not know you, 5
nor I am not sent to you by my lady to bid you come
speak with her, nor your name is not Master Cesario,
nor this is not my nose neither. Nothing that is so is so.

SEBASTIAN I prithee, vent thy folly somewhere else. 9
Thou know'st not me.

FESTE Vent my folly! He has heard that word of some
great man, and now applies it to a fool. Vent my folly!
I am afraid this great lubber, the world, will prove a 13
cockney. I prithee now, ungird thy strangeness and 14
tell me what I shall vent to my lady. Shall I vent to her
that thou art coming?

SEBASTIAN I prithee, foolish Greek, depart from me. 17
There's money for thee. [*He gives money.*] If you tarry
longer, I shall give worse payment.

FESTE By my troth, thou hast an open hand. These 20
wise men that give fools money get themselves a good
report—after fourteen years' purchase. 22

Enter [Sir] Andrew, [Sir] Toby, and Fabian.

SIR ANDREW Now, sir, have I met you again? There's
for you! [*He strikes Sebastian.*]

SEBASTIAN Why, there's for thee, and there, and there!
[*He beats Sir Andrew with the hilt of his dagger.*]
Are all the people mad?

SIR TOBY Hold, sir, or I'll throw your dagger o'er the
house.

FESTE This will I tell my lady straight. I would not be 29
in some of your coats for twopence. [*Exit.*]

4.1. Location: Before Olivia's house.
5 held out kept up   **9 vent** give vent to   **13 lubber** lout   **14 cockney**
effeminate or foppish fellow.   **ungird thy strangeness** put off your
affectation of being a stranger   **17 Greek** i.e., buffoon. (From "merry
Greek.")   **20 open** generous   **22 after . . . purchase** i.e., at great cost.
(Land was ordinarily valued at the price of twelve years' rental; the Fool
adds two years to this figure.)   **29 straight** at once

SIR TOBY   Come on, sir, hold!   [*He grips Sebastian.*]

SIR ANDREW   Nay, let him alone. I'll go another way to
work with him; I'll have an action of battery against   33
him, if there be any law in Illyria. Though I struck him
first, yet it's no matter for that.

SEBASTIAN   Let go thy hand!

SIR TOBY   Come, sir, I will not let you go. Come, my
young soldier, put up your iron. You are well fleshed;   38
come on.

SEBASTIAN

I will be free from thee. [*He breaks free and draws his
   sword.*] What wouldst thou now?
If thou dar'st tempt me further, draw thy sword.

SIR TOBY   What, what? Nay, then I must have an ounce
or two of this malapert blood from you.   [*He draws.*]   43

   Enter Olivia.

OLIVIA

Hold, Toby! On thy life I charge thee, hold!

SIR TOBY   Madam—

OLIVIA

Will it be ever thus? Ungracious wretch,
Fit for the mountains and the barbarous caves,
Where manners ne'er were preached! Out of my sight!
Be not offended, dear Cesario.
Rudesby, begone!
      [*Exeunt Sir Toby, Sir Andrew, and Fabian.*]
               I prithee, gentle friend,   50
Let thy fair wisdom, not thy passion, sway
In this uncivil and unjust extent   52
Against thy peace. Go with me to my house,
And hear thou there how many fruitless pranks
This ruffian hath botched up, that thou thereby   55
Mayst smile at this. Thou shalt not choose but go.
Do not deny. Beshrew his soul for me!   57
He started one poor heart of mine, in thee.   58

---

33 action of battery lawsuit for beating (me)   **38 fleshed** initiated into
battle   **43 malapert** saucy, impudent   **50 Rudesby** ruffian   **52 extent**
attack   **55 botched up** clumsily contrived   **57 Beshrew** curse   **58 He**
. . . **thee** i.e., he alarmed half of my heart, which lies in your bosom.
(The word *started* also suggests a play on *heart, hart.*)

SEBASTIAN [*Aside*]
  What relish is in this? How runs the stream?
  Or I am mad, or else this is a dream.   60
  Let fancy still my sense in Lethe steep;   61
  If it be thus to dream, still let me sleep!
OLIVIA
  Nay, come, I prithee. Would thou'dst be ruled by me!
SEBASTIAN
  Madam, I will.
OLIVIA   O, say so, and so be!   *Exeunt.*

❖

4.2   *Enter Maria [with garments] and Clown [Feste].*

MARIA   Nay, I prithee, put on this gown and this beard;
  make him believe thou art Sir Topas the curate. Do it   2
  quickly. I'll call Sir Toby the whilst.   [*Exit.*]   3
FESTE   Well, I'll put it on, and I will dissemble myself   4
  in 't, and I would I were the first that ever dissembled
  in such a gown. [*He disguises himself in gown and*
  beard.] I am not tall enough to become the function   7
  well, nor lean enough to be thought a good student;   8
  but to be said an honest man and a good housekeeper   9
  goes as fairly as to say a careful man and a great
  scholar. The competitors enter.   11

     Enter [Sir] Toby [and Maria].

SIR TOBY   Jove bless thee, Master Parson.

60 Or either   **61 fancy** imagination.   **still** ever.   **Lethe** the river of forgetfulness in the underworld; i.e., forgetfulness
4.2. Location: Olivia's house.
2 Sir (Honorific title for priests.)   **Topas** (A name perhaps derived from Chaucer's comic knight in the "Rime of Sir Thopas" or from a similar character in Lyly's *Endymion.* Topaz, a semiprecious stone, was believed to be a cure for lunacy.)   **3 the whilst** in the meantime   **4 dissemble** disguise (with a play on "feign")   **7 become** grace, adorn. **function** profession   **8 student** scholar (in divinity)   **9 said** called, known as.   **housekeeper** household manager, hospitable person
11 competitors associates, partners

FESTE   *Bonos dies*, Sir Toby. For, as the old hermit of   13
Prague, that never saw pen and ink, very wittily said   14
to a niece of King Gorboduc, "That that is, is"; so I,   15
being Master Parson, am Master Parson; for what is
"that" but "that," and "is" but "is"?

SIR TOBY   To him, Sir Topas.

FESTE   What, ho, I say! Peace in this prison!

> [*He approaches the door
> behind which Malvolio is confined.*]

SIR TOBY   The knave counterfeits well; a good knave.

MALVOLIO   (*Within*) Who calls there?

FESTE   Sir Topas the curate, who comes to visit Malvolio the lunatic.

MALVOLIO   Sir Topas, Sir Topas, good Sir Topas, go to
my lady—

FESTE   Out, hyperbolical fiend! How vexest thou this   26
man! Talkest thou nothing but of ladies?

SIR TOBY   Well said, Master Parson.

MALVOLIO   Sir Topas, never was man thus wronged.
Good Sir Topas, do not think I am mad. They have
laid me here in hideous darkness.

FESTE   Fie, thou dishonest Satan! I call thee by the
most modest terms, for I am one of those gentle ones
that will use the devil himself with courtesy. Sayst
thou that house is dark?   35

MALVOLIO   As hell, Sir Topas.

FESTE   Why, it hath bay windows transparent as bar-   37
ricadoes, and the clerestories toward the south north   38
are as lustrous as ebony; and yet complainest thou of
obstruction?

MALVOLIO   I am not mad, Sir Topas. I say to you this
house is dark.

FESTE   Madman, thou errest. I say there is no darkness but ignorance, in which thou art more puzzled
than the Egyptians in their fog.   45

---

13 Bonos dies good day   **13–14 hermit of Prague** (Probably another invented authority.)   **15 King Gorboduc** a legendary king of ancient Britain,
protagonist in the English tragedy *Gorbobuc* (1562)   **26 hyperbolical**
vehement, boisterous.   **fiend** i.e., the devil supposedly possessing Malvolio   **35 house** i.e., room   **37–38 barricadoes** barricades   **38 clerestories**
windows in an upper wall   **45 Egyptians . . . fog** (Alluding to the darkness
brought upon Egypt by Moses; see Exodus 10:21–23.)

MALVOLIO   I say this house is as dark as ignorance,
though ignorance were as dark as hell; and I say there
was never man thus abused. I am no more mad than
you are. Make the trial of it in any constant question.   49

FESTE   What is the opinion of Pythagoras concerning   50
wildfowl?   51

MALVOLIO   That the soul of our grandam might haply   52
inhabit a bird.

FESTE   What think'st thou of his opinion?

MALVOLIO   I think nobly of the soul, and no way ap-
prove his opinion.

FESTE   Fare thee well. Remain thou still in darkness.
Thou shalt hold th' opinion of Pythagoras ere I will
allow of thy wits, and fear to kill a woodcock lest thou   59
dispossess the soul of thy grandam. Fare thee well.
                   [He moves away from Malvolio's prison.]

MALVOLIO   Sir Topas, Sir Topas!

SIR TOBY   My most exquisite Sir Topas!

FESTE   Nay, I am for all waters.   63

MARIA   Thou mightst have done this without thy beard
and gown. He sees thee not.

SIR TOBY   To him in thine own voice, and bring me
word how thou find'st him. I would we were well rid
of this knavery. If he may be conveniently delivered, I   68
would he were, for I am now so far in offense with
my niece that I cannot pursue with any safety this
sport to the upshot.—Come by and by to my chamber.   71
                                    Exit [with Maria].

FESTE [Singing as he approaches Malvolio's prison]
         "Hey, Robin, jolly Robin,   72
         Tell me how thy lady does."   73

MALVOLIO   Fool!

FESTE   "My lady is unkind, pardie."   75

MALVOLIO   Fool!

---

49 constant question set problem   **50–51 Pythagoras . . . wildfowl** (An
opening for the discussion of transmigration of souls, a doctrine held by
Pythagoras.)   **52 haply** perhaps   **59 allow of thy wits** i.e., certify your
sanity.   **woodcock** (A proverbially stupid bird, easily caught.)   **63 for all
waters** i.e., ready for anything   **68 delivered** i.e., delivered from prison
71 upshot conclusion   **72–73 Hey, Robin . . . does** (Another fragment of
an old song, a version of which is attributed to Sir Thomas Wyatt.)
75 pardie i.e., by God, certainly

FESTE　"Alas, why is she so?"

MALVOLIO　Fool, I say!

FESTE　"She loves another—" Who calls, ha?

MALVOLIO　Good Fool, as ever thou wilt deserve well at
my hand, help me to a candle, and pen, ink, and paper. As I am a gentleman, I will live to be thankful to
thee for 't.

FESTE　Master Malvolio?

MALVOLIO　Ay, good Fool.

FESTE　Alas, sir, how fell you beside your five wits?　86

MALVOLIO　Fool, there was never man so notoriously
abused. I am as well in my wits, Fool, as thou art.

FESTE　But as well? Then you are mad indeed, if you
be no better in your wits than a fool.

MALVOLIO　They have here propertied me, keep me in　91
darkness, send ministers to me—asses!—and do all
they can to face me out of my wits.　93

FESTE　Advise you what you say. The minister is here.　94
[*He speaks as Sir Topas.*] Malvolio, Malvolio, thy wits
the heavens restore! Endeavor thyself to sleep, and
leave thy vain bibble-babble.

MALVOLIO　Sir Topas!

FESTE [*In Sir Topas's voice*]　Maintain no words with him,
good fellow. [*In his own voice.*] Who, I, sir? Not I,
sir. God b' wi' you, good Sir Topas. [*In Sir Topas's voice.*]　101
Marry, amen. [*In his own voice.*] I will, sir, I will.

MALVOLIO　Fool! Fool! Fool, I say!

FESTE　Alas, sir, be patient. What say you, sir? I am
shent for speaking to you.　105

MALVOLIO　Good Fool, help me to some light and some
paper. I tell thee I am as well in my wits as any man
in Illyria.

FESTE　Welladay that you were, sir!　109

MALVOLIO　By this hand, I am. Good Fool, some ink,

---

86 beside out of.　**five wits** (The intellectual faculties, usually listed as
common wit, imagination, fantasy, judgment, and memory.)　**91 propertied me** i.e., treated me as property and thrown me into the lumber-
room　**93 face . . . wits** brazenly represent me as having lost my wits
94 Advise you take care　**101 God b' wi' you** God be with you. (Feste
uses two voices in this passage to carry on a dialogue between himself
and "Sir Topas.")　**105 shent** scolded, rebuked　**109 Welladay** alas,
would that

paper, and light; and convey what I will set down to
my lady. It shall advantage thee more than ever the
bearing of letter did.

FESTE I will help you to 't. But tell me true, are you
not mad indeed, or do you but counterfeit?

MALVOLIO Believe me, I am not. I tell thee true.

FESTE Nay, I'll ne'er believe a madman till I see his
brains. I will fetch you light and paper and ink.

MALVOLIO Fool, I'll requite it in the highest degree. I
prithee, begone.

FESTE [Sings]
    I am gone, sir,
    And anon, sir,
  I'll be with you again,
    In a trice,
    Like to the old Vice,   125
  Your need to sustain;

    Who, with dagger of lath,   127
    In his rage and his wrath,
  Cries "Aha!" to the devil;
    Like a mad lad,
    "Pare thy nails, dad?
  Adieu, goodman devil!"   *Exit.* 132

❖

4.3   *Enter Sebastian [with a pearl].*

SEBASTIAN
This is the air; that is the glorious sun;
This pearl she gave me, I do feel 't and see 't;
And though 'tis wonder that enwraps me thus,
Yet 'tis not madness. Where's Antonio, then?
I could not find him at the Elephant;
Yet there he was, and there I found this credit,   6
That he did range the town to seek me out.

125 **Vice** comic tempter of the morality plays   127 **dagger of lath** comic
weapon of the Vice   132 **goodman** title for a person of substance but
not of gentle birth

4.3. Location: Olivia's garden.
6 **was** was previously.   **credit** report

His counsel now might do me golden service;
For though my soul disputes well with my sense   9
That this may be some error, but no madness,
Yet doth this accident and flood of fortune
So far exceed all instance, all discourse,   12
That I am ready to distrust mine eyes
And wrangle with my reason that persuades me
To any other trust but that I am mad,   15
Or else the lady's mad. Yet if 'twere so,
She could not sway her house, command her followers,   17
Take and give back affairs and their dispatch,   18
With such a smooth, discreet, and stable bearing
As I perceive she does. There's something in 't
That is deceivable. But here the lady comes.   21

    Enter Olivia and Priest.

OLIVIA
Blame not this haste of mine. If you mean well,
Now go with me and with this holy man
Into the chantry by. There, before him,   24
And underneath that consecrated roof,
Plight me the full assurance of your faith,
That my most jealous and too doubtful soul   27
May live at peace. He shall conceal it
Whiles you are willing it shall come to note,   29
What time we will our celebration keep   30
According to my birth. What do you say?   31

SEBASTIAN
I'll follow this good man, and go with you,
And having sworn truth, ever will be true.

OLIVIA
Then lead the way, good Father, and heavens so shine
That they may fairly note this act of mine!   *Exeunt.* 35

                            ❖

9 my soul . . . sense i.e., both my rational faculties and my physical
senses come to the conclusion   **12 instance** precedent.   **discourse**
reasoning   **15 trust** belief   **17 sway** rule   **18 Take . . . dispatch** undertake matters of business and see to their execution   **21 deceivable**
deceptive   **24 chantry by** privately endowed chapel nearby   **27 jealous**
anxious, mistrustful.   **doubtful** full of doubts   **29 Whiles** until.   **come
to note** become known   **30 What time** at which time.   **our celebration**
i.e., the actual marriage; what they are about to perform is a binding
betrothal   **31 birth** social position   **35 fairly note** look upon with favor

5.1   *Enter Clown [Feste] and Fabian.*

FABIAN   Now, as thou lov'st me, let me see his letter.

FESTE   Good Master Fabian, grant me another request.

FABIAN   Anything.

FESTE   Do not desire to see this letter.

FABIAN   This is to give a dog and in recompense desire 5
my dog again. 6

Enter Duke [Orsino], Viola, Curio, and lords.

ORSINO   Belong you to the Lady Olivia, friends?

FESTE   Ay, sir, we are some of her trappings. 8

ORSINO   I know thee well. How dost thou, my good fellow?

FESTE   Truly, sir, the better for my foes and the worse 10
for my friends.

ORSINO   Just the contrary; the better for thy friends.

FESTE   No, sir, the worse.

ORSINO   How can that be?

FESTE   Marry, sir, they praise me, and make an ass of
me. Now my foes tell me plainly I am an ass; so that
by my foes, sir, I profit in the knowledge of myself,
and by my friends I am abused; so that, conclusions to 18
be as kisses, if your four negatives make your two af- 19
firmatives, why then the worse for my friends and the 20
better for my foes.

ORSINO   Why, this is excellent.

FESTE   By my troth, sir, no; though it please you to be
one of my friends. 24

ORSINO   Thou shalt not be the worse for me. There's gold.
[He gives a coin.]

FESTE   But that it would be double-dealing, sir, I 26
would you could make it another.

5.1. Location: Before Olivia's house.
5–6 This . . . again (Apparently a reference to a well-known reply of Dr.
Bulleyn when Queen Elizabeth asked for his dog and promised a gift of
his choosing in return.)   8 trappings ornaments, decorations   10 for
because of   18 abused flatteringly deceived   18–20 conclusions . . .
affirmatives i.e., as when a young lady, asked for a kiss, says "no, no"
really meaning "yes, yes"; or, as the four lips of two contrary lovers
come together to make one passionate kiss   24 friends i.e., those who,
according to Feste's syllogism, flatter him   26 But except for the fact.
double-dealing (1) giving twice (2) deceit, duplicity

ORSINO   O, you give me ill counsel.

FESTE   Put your grace in your pocket, sir, for this once,   29
and let your flesh and blood obey it.

ORSINO   Well, I will be so much a sinner to be a double-
dealer. There's another.   [*He gives another coin.*]

FESTE   *Primo, secundo, tertio* is a good play, and the   33
old saying is, the third pays for all. The triplex, sir, is   34
a good tripping measure; or the bells of Saint Bennet,   35
sir, may put you in mind—one, two, three.

ORSINO   You can fool no more money out of me at this
throw. If you will let your lady know I am here to   38
speak with her, and bring her along with you, it may
awake my bounty further.

FESTE   Marry, sir, lullaby to your bounty till I come
again. I go, sir, but I would not have you to think that
my desire of having is the sin of covetousness; but as
you say, sir, let your bounty take a nap, I will awake
it anon.   -   *Exit.*

Enter Antonio and Officers.

VIOLA
Here comes the man, sir, that did rescue me.

ORSINO
That face of his I do remember well,
Yet when I saw it last it was besmeared
As black as Vulcan in the smoke of war.   49
A baubling vessel was he captain of,   50
For shallow draft and bulk unprizable,   51
With which such scatheful grapple did he make   52
With the most noble bottom of our fleet   53
That very envy and the tongue of loss   54

---

29 Put . . . pocket (1) pocket up your virtue, your grace before God
(2) reach in your pocket or purse and show your customary grace or
munificence   **33 play** (Perhaps a children's game or game of dice.)
34 triplex triple time in music   **35 Saint Bennet** church of St. Bene-
dict   **38 throw** (1) time (2) throw of the dice   **49 Vulcan** Roman god of
fire and smith to the other gods; his face was blackened by the fire
50 baubling insignificant, trifling   **51 For** because of.   **draft** depth of
water a ship draws.   **unprizable** of value too slight to be estimated, not
worth taking as a "prize"   **52 scatheful** destructive   **53 bottom** ship
54 very envy i.e., even those who had most reason to hate him, his
enemies.   **loss** i.e., the losers

Cried fame and honor on him. What's the matter?

FIRST OFFICER
Orsino, this is that Antonio
That took the Phoenix and her freight from Candy, 57
And this is he that did the *Tiger* board
When your young nephew Titus lost his leg.
Here in the streets, desperate of shame and state, 60
In private brabble did we apprehend him. 61

VIOLA
He did me kindness, sir, drew on my side,
But in conclusion put strange speech upon me. 63
I know not what 'twas but distraction. 64

ORSINO
Notable pirate, thou saltwater thief,
What foolish boldness brought thee to their mercies
Whom thou in terms so bloody and so dear 67
Hast made thine enemies?

ANTONIO   Orsino, noble sir,
Be pleased that I shake off these names you give me. 69
Antonio never yet was thief or pirate,
Though I confess, on base and ground enough, 71
Orsino's enemy. A witchcraft drew me hither.
That most ingrateful boy there by your side
From the rude sea's enraged and foamy mouth
Did I redeem; a wrack past hope he was. 75
His life I gave him, and did thereto add
My love, without retention or restraint, 77
All his in dedication. For his sake
Did I expose myself—pure for his love— 79
Into the danger of this adverse town, 80
Drew to defend him when he was beset;
Where being apprehended, his false cunning,
Not meaning to partake with me in danger,
Taught him to face me out of his acquaintance 84

---

57 from Candy on her return from Candia, or Crete   **60 desperate . . .
state** recklessly disregarding disgrace and his status as a wanted man
61 brabble brawl   **63 put . . . me** spoke to me strangely   **64 but distraction** unless (it was) madness   **67 dear** costly, grievous   **69 Be pleased
that** allow me to   **71 base and ground** solid grounds   **75 wrack** goods
from a wrecked vessel   **77 retention** reservation   **79 pure** entirely,
purely   **80 Into** unto. **adverse** hostile   **84 face . . . acquaintance**
brazenly deny he knew me

And grew a twenty years' removèd thing   85
While one would wink; denied me mine own purse,   86
Which I had recommended to his use   87
Not half an hour before.

VIOLA How can this be?

ORSINO When came he to this town?

ANTONIO
Today, my lord; and for three months before,
No interim, not a minute's vacancy,
Both day and night did we keep company.

Enter Olivia and attendants.

ORSINO
Here comes the Countess; now heaven walks on earth.
But for thee, fellow—fellow, thy words are madness.
Three months this youth hath tended upon me;
But more of that anon. Take him aside.

OLIVIA
What would my lord—but that he may not have—   98
Wherein Olivia may seem serviceable?
Cesario, you do not keep promise with me.

VIOLA Madam?

ORSINO Gracious Olivia—

OLIVIA
What do you say, Cesario? Good my lord—

VIOLA
My lord would speak; my duty hushes me.

OLIVIA
If it be aught to the old tune, my lord,
It is as fat and fulsome to mine ear   106
As howling after music.

ORSINO Still so cruel?

OLIVIA Still so constant, lord.

ORSINO
What, to perverseness? You uncivil lady,
To whose ingrate and unauspicious altars

85–86 grew . . . wink in the twinkling of an eye acted as though we had
been estranged for twenty years **87 recommended** consigned **98 but
that** except that which. **he . . . have** i.e., my love **106 fat and fulsome**
gross and offensive

My soul the faithfull'st offerings have breathed out
That e'er devotion tendered! What shall I do?

OLIVIA

Even what it please my lord that shall become him.

ORSINO

Why should I not, had I the heart to do it,
Like to th' Egyptian thief at point of death,   116
Kill what I love?—a savage jealousy
That sometimes savors nobly. But hear me this: 118
Since you to nonregardance cast my faith,   119
And that I partly know the instrument
That screws me from my true place in your favor,   121
Live you the marble-breasted tyrant still.
But this your minion, whom I know you love,   123
And whom, by heaven I swear, I tender dearly,   124
Him will I tear out of that cruel eye
Where he sits crownèd in his master's spite.—   126
Come, boy, with me. My thoughts are ripe in mischief.
I'll sacrifice the lamb that I do love,
To spite a raven's heart within a dove.   [*Going.*]

VIOLA

And I, most jocund, apt, and willingly,
To do you rest, a thousand deaths would die.   131
                                                 [*Going.*]

OLIVIA

Where goes Cesario?

VIOLA   After him I love
More than I love these eyes, more than my life,
More by all mores than e'er I shall love wife.   134
If I do feign, you witnesses above
Punish my life for tainting of my love!

OLIVIA

Ay me, detested! How am I beguiled!

---

116 Egyptian thief (An allusion to the story of Theagenes and Chariclea
in the *Ethiopica*, a Greek romance by Heliodorus. The robber chief,
Thyamis of Memphis, having captured Chariclea and fallen in love with
her, is attacked by a larger band of robbers; threatened with death, he
attempts to slay her first.)   **118 savors nobly** is not without nobility
119 nonregardance neglect   **121 screws** pries, forces   **123 minion**
darling, favorite   **124 tender** regard   **126 in . . . spite** in defiance of his
master   **131 do you rest** give you ease   **134 by all mores** by all such
comparisons

VIOLA
  Who does beguile you? Who does do you wrong?
OLIVIA
  Hast thou forgot thyself? Is it so long?
  Call forth the holy father.   [*Exit an Attendant.*]
ORSINO [*To Viola*]   Come, away!
OLIVIA
  Whither, my lord? Cesario, husband, stay.
ORSINO
  Husband?
OLIVIA   Ay, husband. Can he that deny?
ORSINO
  Her husband, sirrah?
VIOLA   No, my lord, not I.
OLIVIA
  Alas, it is the baseness of thy fear
  That makes thee strangle thy propriety.   145
  Fear not, Cesario, take thy fortunes up;
  Be that thou know'st thou art, and then thou art   147
  As great as that thou fear'st.

      Enter Priest.

                        O, welcome, Father!   148
  Father, I charge thee by thy reverence
  Here to unfold, though lately we intended
  To keep in darkness what occasion now
  Reveals before 'tis ripe, what thou dost know
  Hath newly passed between this youth and me.
PRIEST
  A contract of eternal bond of love,
  Confirmed by mutual joinder of your hands,   155
  Attested by the holy close of lips,   156
  Strengthened by interchangement of your rings,
  And all the ceremony of this compact
  Sealed in my function, by my testimony;   159
  Since when, my watch hath told me, toward my grave
  I have traveled but two hours.
ORSINO
  O thou dissembling cub! What wilt thou be

145 strangle thy propriety deny what you are   **147 that** that which
148 that thou fear'st him you fear, i.e., Orsino   **155 joinder** joining
156 close meeting   **159 Sealed** ratified

When time hath sowed a grizzle on thy case?   163
Or will not else thy craft so quickly grow
That thine own trip shall be thine overthrow?   165
Farewell, and take her, but direct thy feet
Where thou and I henceforth may never meet.

VIOLA
My lord, I do protest—

OLIVIA   O, do not swear!
Hold little faith, though thou hast too much fear.   169

  Enter Sir Andrew.

SIR ANDREW For the love of God, a surgeon! Send one
 presently to Sir Toby.

OLIVIA What's the matter?

SIR ANDREW He's broke my head across and has given   173
 Sir Toby a bloody coxcomb too. For the love of God,   174
 your help! I had rather than forty pound I were at
 home.

OLIVIA Who has done this, Sir Andrew?

SIR ANDREW The Count's gentleman, one Cesario. We
 took him for a coward, but he's the very devil incar- 179
 dinate.   180

ORSINO My gentleman, Cesario?

SIR ANDREW 'Od's lifelings, here he is!—You broke my   182
 head for nothing, and that that I did, I was set on to
 do 't by Sir Toby.

VIOLA
Why do you speak to me? I never hurt you.
You drew your sword upon me without cause,
But I bespake you fair, and hurt you not.   187

SIR ANDREW If a bloody coxcomb be a hurt, you have
 hurt me. I think you set nothing by a bloody cox-   189
 comb.

  Enter [Sir] Toby and Clown [Feste].

Here comes Sir Toby halting; you shall hear more. But   191

---

163 a grizzle gray hair. **case** sheath, skin **165 trip** wrestling trick (i.e.,
you'll get overclever, and trip yourself up) **169 little** i.e., a little
173 broke broken the skin, cut **174 coxcomb** fool's cap resembling the
crest of a cock; here, head **179–180 incardinate** (for *incarnate*)
182 'Od's lifelings by God's little lives **187 fair** courteously **189 set
nothing by** regard as insignificant **191 halting** limping

if he had not been in drink, he would have tickled you
othergates than he did.   193

ORSINO   How now, gentleman? How is 't with you?

SIR TOBY   That's all one. He's hurt me, and there's th'
end on 't.—Sot, didst see Dick surgeon, sot?   196

FESTE   O, he's drunk, Sir Toby, an hour agone; his
eyes were set at eight i' the morning.   198

SIR TOBY   Then he's a rogue, and a passy measures   199
pavane. I hate a drunken rogue.   200

OLIVIA   Away with him! Who hath made this havoc
with them?

SIR ANDREW   I'll help you, Sir Toby, because we'll be   203
dressed together.   204

SIR TOBY   Will you help? An ass-head and a coxcomb
and a knave, a thin-faced knave, a gull!

OLIVIA
Get him to bed, and let his hurt be looked to.
            [Exeunt Feste, Fabian, Sir Toby, and Sir
                                        Andrew.]

        Enter Sebastian.

SEBASTIAN
I am sorry, madam, I have hurt your kinsman;
But, had it been the brother of my blood,
I must have done no less with wit and safety.—   210
You throw a strange regard upon me, and by that   211
I do perceive it hath offended you.
Pardon me, sweet one, even for the vows
We made each other but so late ago.

ORSINO
One face, one voice, one habit, and two persons,   215
A natural perspective, that is and is not!   216

SEBASTIAN
Antonio, O my dear Antonio!

193 othergates otherwise   **196 Sot** (1) fool (2) drunkard   **198 set** fixed
or extinguished, closed   **199–200 passy measures pavane** a slow-moving
eight-bar grave and stately dance (suggesting Sir Toby's impatience to
have his wounds dressed)   **203–204 be dressed** i.e., have our wounds
surgically dressed   **210 with wit and safety** with intelligent concern for
my own safety   **211 strange regard** look such as one directs at a stranger
215 habit dress   **216 natural perspective** an optical device or illusion
created by nature

How have the hours racked and tortured me
Since I have lost thee!

ANTONIO   Sebastian are you?

SEBASTIAN   Fear'st thou that, Antonio?   221

ANTONIO
How have you made division of yourself?
An apple cleft in two is not more twin
Than these two creatures. Which is Sebastian?

OLIVIA   Most wonderful!

SEBASTIAN [*Seeing Viola*]
Do I stand there? I never had a brother;
Nor can there be that deity in my nature
Of here and everywhere. I had a sister,   228
Whom the blind waves and surges have devoured.   229
Of charity, what kin are you to me?   230
What countryman? What name? What parentage?

VIOLA
Of Messaline; Sebastian was my father.
Such a Sebastian was my brother too;
So went he suited to his watery tomb.   234
If spirits can assume both form and suit,
You come to fright us.

SEBASTIAN   A spirit I am indeed,
But am in that dimension grossly clad   237
Which from the womb I did participate.   238
Were you a woman, as the rest goes even,   239
I should my tears let fall upon your cheek,
And say "Thrice welcome, drownèd Viola!"

VIOLA
My father had a mole upon his brow.

SEBASTIAN   And so had mine.

VIOLA
And died that day when Viola from her birth
Had numbered thirteen years.

SEBASTIAN
O, that record is lively in my soul!   246

---

221 Fear'st thou that do you doubt that   **228 here and everywhere**
omnipresence   **229 blind** heedless, indiscriminating   **230 Of charity**
(tell me) in kindness   **234 suited** dressed; clad in human form
237 in . . . clad clothed in that fleshly shape   **238 participate** possess
239 as . . . even since everything else agrees   **246 record** recollection

He finishèd indeed his mortal act
That day that made my sister thirteen years.

VIOLA
If nothing lets to make us happy both   249
But this my masculine usurped attire,
Do not embrace me till each circumstance
Of place, time, fortune, do cohere and jump   252
That I am Viola—which to confirm,
I'll bring you to a captain in this town,
Where lie my maiden weeds; by whose gentle help   255
I was preserved to serve this noble count.
All the occurrence of my fortune since
Hath been between this lady and this lord.

SEBASTIAN [*To Olivia*]
So comes it, lady, you have been mistook.
But nature to her bias drew in that.   260
You would have been contracted to a maid;
Nor are you therein, by my life, deceived.
You are betrothed both to a maid and man.   263

ORSINO
Be not amazed; right noble is his blood.
If this be so, as yet the glass seems true,   265
I shall have share in this most happy wrack.   266
[*To Viola.*] Boy, thou hast said to me a thousand times
Thou never shouldst love woman like to me.

VIOLA
And all those sayings will I over swear,   269
And all those swearings keep as true in soul
As doth that orbèd continent the fire   271
That severs day from night.

ORSINO   Give me thy hand,.
And let me see thee in thy woman's weeds.

VIOLA
The captain that did bring me first on shore
Hath my maid's garments. He upon some action   275

---

249 lets hinders   **252 jump** coincide, fit exactly   **255 weeds** clothes
260 nature . . . that nature followed her bent in that   **263 a maid** i.e., a
virgin man   **265 glass** i.e., the *natural perspective* of l. 216   **266 wrack**
goods from a wrecked vessel   **269 over swear** swear again   **271 As . . .**
fire i.e., as the sphere of the sun keeps the fire   **275 action** legal charge

Is now in durance, at Malvolio's suit,   276
A gentleman and follower of my lady's.

OLIVIA

He shall enlarge him. Fetch Malvolio hither.   278
And yet, alas, now I remember me,
They say, poor gentleman, he's much distract.

Enter Clown [Feste] with a letter, and Fabian.

A most extracting frenzy of mine own   281
From my remembrance clearly banished his.
How does he, sirrah?

FESTE   Truly, madam, he holds Belzebub at the stave's   284
end as well as a man in his case may do. He's here   285
writ a letter to you; I should have given 't you today
morning. But as a madman's epistles are no gospels,   287
so it skills not much when they are delivered.   288

OLIVIA   Open 't, and read it.

FESTE   Look then to be well edified, when the fool de-   290
livers the madman. [*Reads loudly.*] "By the Lord,   291
madam—"

OLIVIA   How now, art thou mad?

FESTE   No, madam, I do but read madness. An your
ladyship will have it as it ought to be, you must allow
vox.   296

OLIVIA   Prithee, read i' thy right wits.

FESTE   So I do, madonna; but to read his right wits is
to read thus. Therefore perpend, my princess, and   299
give ear.

OLIVIA [*To Fabian*]   Read it you, sirrah.

FABIAN [*Reads*]   "By the Lord, madam, you wrong me,
and the world shall know it. Though you have put me
into darkness and given your drunken cousin rule
over me, yet have I the benefit of my senses as well as

---

276 durance captivity   **278 enlarge** release   **281 extracting** i.e., that
obsessed me and drew all thoughts except of Cesario from my mind
284–285 holds . . . end i.e., keeps the devil at a safe distance   **287 a
madman's . . . gospels** i.e., there is no truth in a madman's letters. (An
allusion to readings in the church service of selected passages from the
epistles and the gospels.)   **288 skills** matters   **290–291 delivers** speaks
the words of   **296 vox** voice, i.e., an appropriately loud voice   **299 perpend** consider, attend

your ladyship. I have your own letter that induced me
to the semblance I put on, with the which I doubt not   307
but to do myself much right or you much shame.
Think of me as you please. I leave my duty a little
unthought of and speak out of my injury.

                              The madly used Malvolio."

OLIVIA   Did he write this?

FESTE   Ay, madam.

ORSINO   This savors not much of distraction.

OLIVIA
See him delivered, Fabian; bring him hither.   315
                                      [Exit Fabian.]
My lord, so please you, these things further thought on, 316
To think me as well a sister as a wife,   317
One day shall crown th' alliance on 't, so please you, 318
Here at my house and at my proper cost.   319

ORSINO
Madam, I am most apt t' embrace your offer.
[To Viola.] Your master quits you; and for your service
   done him,   321
So much against the mettle of your sex,   322
So far beneath your soft and tender breeding,
And since you called me master for so long,
Here is my hand. You shall from this time be
Your master's mistress.

OLIVIA   A sister! You are she.

      Enter [Fabian, with] Malvolio.

ORSINO
Is this the madman?

OLIVIA   Ay, my lord, this same.
How now, Malvolio?

MALVOLIO   Madam, you have done me wrong,
Notorious wrong.

OLIVIA   Have I, Malvolio? No.

---

307 the which i.e., the letter **315 delivered** released **316 so . . . on** if
you are pleased on further consideration **317 To . . . wife** to regard
me as favorably as a sister-in-law as you had hoped to regard me as a
wife **318 crown . . . on 't** i.e., serve as occasion for two marriages
confirming our new relationship **319 proper** own **321 quits** releases
322 mettle natural disposition

MALVOLIO

Lady, you have. Pray you, peruse that letter.

                     [*He gives letter.*]

You must not now deny it is your hand.

Write from it, if you can, in hand or phrase,   332

Or say 'tis not your seal, not your invention.   333

You can say none of this. Well, grant it then,

And tell me, in the modesty of honor,   335

Why you have given me such clear lights of favor,

Bade me come smiling and cross-gartered to you,

To put on yellow stockings, and to frown

Upon Sir Toby and the lighter people?   339

And, acting this in an obedient hope,

Why have you suffered me to be imprisoned,

Kept in a dark house, visited by the priest,

And made the most notorious geck and gull   343

That e'er invention played on? Tell me why?   344

OLIVIA

Alas, Malvolio, this is not my writing,

Though, I confess, much like the character;   346

But out of question 'tis Maria's hand.   347

And now I do bethink me, it was she

First told me thou wast mad; then cam'st in smiling,   349

And in such forms which here were presupposed   350

Upon thee in the letter. Prithee, be content.

This practice hath most shrewdly passed upon thee;   352

But when we know the grounds and authors of it,

Thou shalt be both the plaintiff and the judge

Of thine own cause.

FABIAN   Good madam, hear me speak,

And let no quarrel nor no brawl to come

Taint the condition of this present hour,

Which I have wondered at. In hope it shall not,

Most freely I confess, myself and Toby

Set this device against Malvolio here,

---

332 from it differently   **333 invention** composition   **335 modesty of honor** sense of propriety belonging to honorable persons   **339 lighter** lesser   **343 geck** dupe   **344 invention** contrivance   **346 character** handwriting   **347 out of** beyond   **349 cam'st** you came   **350 presupposed** specified beforehand   **352 shrewdly** cruelly, grievously. **passed upon** imposed on

Upon some stubborn and uncourteous parts   361
We had conceived against him. Maria writ   362
The letter at Sir Toby's great importance,   363
In recompense whereof he hath married her.
How with a sportful malice it was followed   365
May rather pluck on laughter than revenge,   366
If that the injuries be justly weighed
That have on both sides passed.

OLIVIA
Alas, poor fool, how have they baffled thee!   369

FESTE Why, "some are born great, some achieve
greatness, and some have greatness thrown upon
them." I was one, sir, in this interlude, one Sir Topas,   372
sir, but that's all one. "By the Lord, Fool, I am not
mad." But do you remember? "Madam, why laugh
you at such a barren rascal? An you smile not, he's
gagged." And thus the whirligig of time brings in his   376
revenges.

MALVOLIO I'll be revenged on the whole pack of you!
                                                  [Exit.]

OLIVIA
He hath been most notoriously abused.

ORSINO
Pursue him, and entreat him to a peace.
He hath not told us of the captain yet.
When that is known, and golden time convents,   382
A solemn combination shall be made
Of our dear souls. Meantime, sweet sister,
We will not part from hence. Cesario, come—
For so you shall be, while you are a man;
But when in other habits you are seen,
Orsino's mistress and his fancy's queen.
                          Exeunt [all, except Feste].

FESTE (Sings)
     When that I was and a little tiny boy,
          With hey, ho, the wind and the rain,

361 Upon on account of. parts qualities, deeds 362 conceived against
him seen and resented in him 363 importance importunity 365 followed carried out 366 pluck on induce 369 baffled disgraced,
quelled 372 interlude little play 376 whirligig spinning top 382 convents (1) summons, calls together (2) suits

A foolish thing was but a toy,
　　For the rain it raineth every day.

But when I came to man's estate,
　　With hey, ho, the wind and the rain,
'Gainst knaves and thieves men shut their gate,
　　For the rain it raineth every day.

But when I came, alas, to wive,
　　With hey, ho, the wind and the rain,
By swaggering could I never thrive,
　　For the rain it raineth every day.

But when I came unto my beds,
　　With hey, ho, the wind and the rain,
With tosspots still had drunken heads,　　　403
　　For the rain it raineth every day.

A great while ago the world begun,
　　With hey, ho, the wind and the rain,
But that's all one, our play is done,
　　And we'll strive to please you every day.

　　　　　　　　　　　　　　[*Exit.*]

403 tosspots drunkards

Date and Text

Twelfth Night was registered with the London Company of Stationers (booksellers and printers) in 1623 and first published in the First Folio that year in a good text set up from what may have been a scribal transcript of Shakespeare's foul papers, or draft manuscript. There was a brief delay in printing *Twelfth Night* in the First Folio, possibly because a transcript was being prepared. The play was first mentioned, however, on Candlemas Day, February 2, 1602, in the following entry from the *Diary* of a Middle Temple (one of the Inns of Court, where law was studied) law student or barrister named John Manningham:

> At our feast wee had a play called "Twelue Night, or What you Will," much like the Commedy of Errores, or Menechmi in Plautus, but most like and neere to that in Italian called *Inganni*. A good practise in it to make the Steward beleeve his Lady widdowe was in love with him, by counterfeyting a letter as from his Lady in generall termes, telling him what shee liked best in him, and prescribing his gesture in smiling, his apparaile, & c., and then when he came to practise making him beleeue they tooke him to be mad.

This entry was once suspected to be a forgery perpetrated by John Payne Collier, who published the *Diary* in 1831, but its authenticity is now generally accepted. The date accords with several possible allusions in the play itself. When Fabian jokes about "a pension of thousands to be paid from the Sophy" (2.5.176–177), he seems to be recalling Sir Anthony Shirley's reception by the Shah of Persia (the Sophy) in 1599–1600. An account of this visit was entered in the Stationers' Register in November of 1601. Viola's description of Feste as "wise enough to play the fool" (3.1.60) may recall a poem beginning "True it is, he plays the fool indeed" published in 1600–1601 by Robert Armin (who had played the role of Feste). Maria's comparison of Malvolio's smiling face to "the new map with the augmentation of the Indies" (3.2.77–78) refers to new maps of about 1600 in which America (the Indies) was increased in size. Leslie Hotson (*The First Night of Twelfth Night*, 1954) has argued for a first performance at court on Twelfth Night in January of 1601, when Queen Elizabeth entertained Don Virginio Orsino, Duke of Bracciano, but this hypothesis has not gained general acceptance partly because the role of Orsino in the play would scarcely flatter such a noble visitor and partly because there is no proof that any of Shakespeare's plays were originally commissioned for private performance. Nevertheless, a date between 1600 and early 1602 seems most likely. Francis Meres does not mention the play in 1598 in his *Palladis Tamia: Wit's Treasury* (a slender volume on contemporary literature and art; valuable because it lists most of Shakespeare's plays that existed at that time).

Textual Notes

These textual notes are not a historical collation, either of the early folios or of more recent editions; they are simply a record of departures in this edition from the copy text. The reading adopted in this edition appears in boldface, followed by the rejected reading from the copy text, i.e., the First Folio. Only a few major alterations in punctuation are noted. Changes in lineation are not indicated, nor are some minor and obvious typographical errors.

Abbreviations used:
F the First Folio
s.d. stage direction
s.p. speech prefix

Copy Text: the First Folio.

1.1. 1 s.p. [and throughout] Orsino Duke   **11 sea, naught** sea. Nought

1.2. 15 Arion Orion

1.3. 51 s.p. Sir Andrew Ma   **54 Mary Accost** Mary, accost   **96 curl by** coole my   **98 me** we   **132 dun** dam'd.   **set** sit   **136 That's** That

1.5. 5 s.p. [and throughout] Feste Clown   **163 s.d. Viola** Uiolenta **296 County's** Countes   **306 s.d.** [F adds "Finis, Actus primus"]

2.2. 31 our O   **32 of** if

2.3. 25 leman Lemon

2.4. 51 s.p. Feste [not in F]   **53 Fly . . . fly** Fye . . . fie   **55 yew** Ew   **88 I** It

2.5. 112 staniel stallion   **118 portend?** portend,   **142 born** become.   **achieve** atcheeues   **173 dear** deero   **203 s.d.** [F adds "Finis Actus secundus"]

3.1. 8 king Kings   **68 wise men** wisemens   **91 all ready** already

3.2. 7 thee the the   **64 nine** mine

3.4. 15 s.d. [at l. 14 in F]   **25 s.p. Olivia** Mal   **65 s.d. Exeunt** Exit   **72 tang** langer   **175 You** Yon   **222 thee** the   **249 competent** computent   **312 s.d.** [at l. 311 in F]   **397 s.d. Exeunt** Exit

4.2. 6 in in in   **38 clerestories** cleere stores   **71 sport to** sport

4.3. 1 s.p. Sebastian [not in F]   **35 s.d.** [F adds "Finis Actus Quartus"]

5.1. 190 s.d. [at l. 187 in F]   **200 pavane** panyn   **205 help? An** helpe an **389 tiny** tine   **406 With hey** hey

Shakespeare's Sources

John Manningham's description of a performance of *Twelfth Night* on February 2, 1602, at the Middle Temple (one of the Inns of Court, where young men studied law in London), compares the play to Plautus' *The Menaechmi* and to an Italian play called *Inganni*. The comment offers a helpful hint on sources. *The Menaechmi* had been the chief source for Shakespeare's earlier play *The Comedy of Errors*, and that farce of mistaken identity clearly resembles *Twelfth Night* in the hilarious mixups resulting from the confusion of two look-alike twins. Shakespeare clearly profited from his earlier experimenting with this sort of comedy. *Twelfth Night* is not necessarily directly indebted to *The Menaechmi*, however, for Renaissance Italian comedy offered many imitations of Plautus from which Shakespeare could have taken his *Twelfth Night* plot. These include *Gl'Inganni* (1562) by Nicolò Secchi, another *Gl'Inganni* (1592) by Curzio Gonzaga, and most important an anonymous *Gl'Ingannati* (published 1537). This last play was translated into French by Charles Estienne as *Les Abusés* (1543) and adapted into Spanish by Lope de Rueda in *Los Engaños* (1567). A Latin version, *Laelia*, based on the French, was performed at Cambridge in the 1590s but never printed. Obviously, *Gl'Ingannati* was widely known, and Manningham was probably referring to it in his diary. To trace Shakespeare's own reading in this matter is difficult, owing to the large number of versions available to him, but we can note the suggestive points of comparison in each.

Both *Inganni* plays feature a brother and a sister mistaken for one another. In the later play (by Gonzaga), the sister uses the disguise name of "Cesare." In Secchi's *Inganni* the disguised sister is in love with her master, who is told that a woman the exact age of his supposed page is secretly in love with him. Another play by Secchi, *L'Interesse* (1581), has a comic duel involving a disguised heroine. Of the Italian plays considered here, however, *Gl'Ingannati* is closest to Shakespeare's play. A short prefatory entertainment included with it in most editions features the name Malevolti. In the play itself, the heroine, Lelia, disguises herself as a page in the service of Flaminio, whom she secretly loves, and is sent on embassies to Flaminio's disdainful mistress Isabella. This lady falls in love with "Fabio," as Lelia calls herself. Lelia's father, Virginio, learning of her disguise and resolving to marry her to old Gherardo (Isabella's father), seeks out Lelia but instead mistakenly arrests her long-lost twin brother, Fabrizio, who has just arrived in Modena. Fabrizio is locked up as a mad person in Isabella's room, whereupon Isabella takes the opportunity to betroth herself to the person she mistakes for "Fabio." A recognition scene clears up everything and leads to the marriages of Fabrizio to Isabella and Flaminio to Lelia. This story lacks the subplot of Malvolio, Sir Toby, et al. Nor is there a shipwreck.

Matteo Bandello based one of the stories in his *Novelle* (1554) on *Gl'Ingannati*, and this prose version was then translated into French by François de Belleforest in his *Histoires Tragiques* (1579 edition). Shakespeare may well have read both, for he consulted these collections of stories in writing *Much Ado about Nothing*. His most direct source, however, seems to have been the story of "Apollonius and Silla," by Barnabe Riche (an English soldier and fiction writer), in *Riche His Farewell to Military Profession* (1581), which was derived from Belleforest. A full modernized text of Riche's story appears in the following pages. Riche involves his characters in more serious moral predicaments than Shakespeare allows in his festive comedy. The plot situation is much the same: Silla (the equivalent of Shakespeare's Viola) is washed ashore near Constantinople, where, disguised as "Silvio," she takes service with a duke, Apollonius (Shakespeare's Orsino), and goes on embassies to the wealthy widow Julina (Shakespeare's Olivia), who proceeds at once to fall in love with "Silvio." When Silla's twin brother, the real Silvio, arrives, he is mistaken by Julina for his twin and is invited to a rendezvous, like Shakespeare's Sebastian. The differences at this point are marked, however, for Silvio becomes Julina's lover and leaves her pregnant when he departs the next day on his quest for Silla. Apollonius is understandably furious to learn of "Silvio's" apparent success with Julina and throws his page into prison. Julina is no less distressed when she learns that the supposed father of her child is in actuality a woman. Only Silla's revelation of her identity and Silvio's eventual return to marry Julina resolves these complications. Shakespeare eschews the pregnancy, the desertion, the imprisonment, and all of Riche's stern moralizings about the bestiality of lust that accompany this lurid tale. Moreover he adds the plot of Malvolio, for which Riche provides little suggestion. Shakespeare changes the location to Illyria, with its hint of delirium and illusion, and provides an English flavor in the comic scenes that intensifies the festive character of the play.

Shakespeare's reading may also have included the anonymous play *Sir Clyomon and Sir Clamydes* (c. 1570–1583), Sir Philip Sidney's *Arcadia* (1590), and Emmanuel Forde's prose romance *Parismus* (1598) in which one "Violetta" borrows the disguise of a page. Scholars have suggested that the Malvolio plot may reflect an incident at Queen Elizabeth's court in which the Comptroller of the Household, Sir William Knollys, interrupted a noisy late-night party dressed in only his nightshirt and a pair of spectacles, with a copy of the Italian pornographic writer Aretino's work in his hand. A similar confrontation between revelry and sobriety occurred in 1598: Ambrose Willoughby quieted a disturbance after the Queen had gone to bed, and was afterward thanked by her for doing his duty. Such incidents were no doubt common, however, and there is no compelling reason to suppose Shakespeare was sketching from current court gossip.

Riche His Farewell to Military Profession
Barnabe Riche

APOLLONIUS AND SILLA

Apollonius, Duke, having spent a year's service in the wars against the Turk, returning homeward with his company by sea, was driven by force of weather to the isle of Cyprus, where he was well received by Pontus, governor of the same isle; with whom Silla, daughter to Pontus, fell so strangely in love that after Apollonius was departed to Constantinople, Silla, with one man, followed. And coming to Constantinople she served Apollonius in the habit of a man; and after many pretty accidents falling out she was known to Apollonius, who, in requital of her love, married her.

There is no child that is born into this wretched world but, before it doth suck the mother's milk, it taketh first a sip* of the cup of error, which maketh us, when we come to riper years, not only to enter into actions of injury but many times to stray from that[1] is right and reason. But in[2] all other things wherein we show ourselves to be most drunken with this poisoned cup, it is in our actions of love. For the lover is so estranged from that[3] is right and wandereth so wide from the bounds of reason that he is not able to deem[4] white from black, good from bad, virtue from vice; but, only led[5] by the appetite of his own affections, and grounding them on the foolishness of his own fancies, will so settle his liking on such a one as either by desert or unworthiness will merit rather to be loathed than loved.

If a question might be asked, what is the ground indeed of reasonable love whereby the knot is knit of true and perfect friendship, I think those that be wise would answer: desert.[6] That is, where the party beloved doth requite us with the like. For otherwise, if the bare show of beauty or the comeliness of personage might be sufficient to confirm us in our love, those that be accustomed to go to fairs and

---

1 **that** that which   2 **But in** i.e., but more than in   3 **that** that which
4 **deem** distinguish   5 **only led** led only   6 **desert** deserving of recompense, offering something in return

markets might sometimes fall into love with twenty in a day. Desert must then be, of force,[7] the ground of reasonable love; for to love them that hate us, to follow them that fly from us, to fawn on them that frown on us, to curry favor with them that disdain us, to be glad to please them that care not how they offend us—who will not confess this to be an erroneous love, neither grounded upon wit nor reason? Wherefore, right courteous gentlewomen, if it please you with patience to peruse this history following, you shall see Dame Error so play her part with a leash[8] of lovers, a male and two females, as shall work a wonder to your wise judgment in noting the effect of their amorous devices and conclusions of their actions: the first neglecting the love of a noble dame, young, beautiful, and fair, who only for his good will[9] played the part of a servingman, contented to abide any manner of pain only to behold him. He again setting his love of[10] a dame that, despising him, being a noble duke, gave herself to a servingman, as she had thought. But it otherwise fell out, as the substance of this tale shall better describe. And because I have been something[11] tedious in my first discourse, offending your patient ears with the hearing of a circumstance[12] overlong, from henceforth that which I mind[13] to write shall be done with such celerity as the matter that I pretend to pen[14] may in any wise permit me. And thus followeth the history.

During the time that the famous city of Constantinople remained in the hands of the Christians, amongst many other noblemen that kept their abiding in that flourishing city there was one whose name was Apollonius, a worthy duke, who, being but a very young man and even then new come to his possessions, which were very great, levied a mighty band of men at his own proper charges,[15] with whom he served against the Turk during the space of one whole year; in which time, although it were very short, this young duke so behaved himself, as well by prowess and valiance showed with his own hands as otherwise by his wisdom and liberality used towards his soldiers, that all the

7 **of force** of necessity   8 **leash** set of three. (Said of hounds, hawks, etc.)
9 **for his good will** to obtain his affection   10 **setting his love of** fixing
his love on   11 **something** somewhat   12 **a circumstance** an incident
13 **mind** intend   14 **pretend to pen** set forth, profess to write   15 **his own proper charges** his own expense

world was filled with the fame of this noble duke. When he had thus spent one year's service, he caused his trumpet to sound a retreat, and gathering his company together and embarking themselves, he set sail, holding his course towards Constantinople. But being upon the sea, by the extremity of a tempest which suddenly fell, his fleet was dissevered, some one way and some another; but he himself recovered[16] the isle of Cyprus, where he was worthily received by Pontus, duke and governor of the same isle, with whom he lodged while his ships were new repairing.

This Pontus, that was lord and governor of this famous isle, was an ancient[17] duke, and had two children, a son and a daughter. His son was named Silvio, of whom hereafter we shall have further occasion to speak; but at this instant he was in the parts of Africa, serving in the wars.

The daughter her[18] name was Silla, whose beauty was so peerless that she had the sovereignty amongst all other dames as well for her beauty as for the nobleness of her birth. This Silla, having heard of the worthiness of Apollonius, this young duke, who besides his beauty and good graces had a certain natural allurement, that, being now in his company in her father's court, she was so strangely attached with the love of Apollonius that there was nothing might content her but his presence and sweet sight. And although she saw no manner of hope to attain to that she most desired—knowing Apollonius to be but a guest and ready to take the benefit of the next wind and to depart into a strange country, whereby she was bereaved of all possibility ever to see him again, and therefore strived with herself to leave her fondness,[19] but all in vain—it would not be, but like the fowl which is once limed,[20] the more she striveth the faster she tieth herself. So Silla was now constrained, perforce[21] her will, to yield to love. Wherefore from time to time she used so great familiarity with him as her honor might well permit, and fed him with such amorous baits as the modesty of a maid could reasonably afford; which when she perceived did take but small effect, feeling herself so much outraged[22] with the extremity of her passion, by the

16 recovered reached   **17 ancient** of ancient family   **18 daughter her** daughter's   **19 fondness** doting   **20 limed** caught with sticky lime placed on a branch   **21 perforce** contrary to   **22 so much outraged** driven to such an intemperate passion

only countenance that she bestowed upon Apollonius it might have been well perceived that the very eyes pleaded unto him for pity and remorse. But Apollonius, coming but lately from out the field from the chasing of his enemies, and his fury not yet thoroughly dissolved nor purged from his stomach, gave no regard to those amorous enticements which, by reason of his youth, he had not been acquainted withal.[23] But his mind ran more to hear his pilots bring news of a merry[24] wind to serve his turn to Constantinople, which in the end came very prosperously; and giving Duke Pontus hearty thanks for his great entertainment, taking his leave of himself and the lady Silla, his daughter, departed with his company, and with a happy[25] gale arrived at his desired port.

Gentlewomen, according to my promise, I will here, for brevity's sake, omit to make repetition of the long and dolorous discourse recorded by Silla for this sudden departure of her Apollonius, knowing you to be as tenderly hearted as Silla herself, whereby you may the better conjecture the fury of her fever. But Silla, the further that she saw herself bereaved of all hope ever any more to see her beloved Apollonius, so much the more contagious were her passions, and made the greater speed to execute that[26] she had premeditated in her mind, which was this. Amongst many servants that did attend upon her, there was one whose name was Pedro, who had a long time waited upon her in her chamber, whereby she was well assured of his fidelity and trust; to that Pedro therefore she bewrayed[27] first the fervency of her love borne to Apollonius, conjuring him in the name of the Goddess of Love herself and binding him by the duty that a servant ought to have that tendereth[28] his mistress's safety and good liking, and desiring him, with tears trickling down her cheeks, that he would give his consent to aid and assist her in that[29] she had determined, which was for that[30] she was fully resolved to go to Constantinople, where she might again take the view of her beloved Apollonius; that he,[31] according to the trust she had reposed in him, would not refuse to give his consent secretly to con-

23 **withal** with   24 **merry** pleasant, favorable   25 **happy** prosperous
26 **that** what   27 **bewrayed** revealed   28 **tendereth** has a tender regard
for, holds dearly   29 **that** what   30 **for that** that   31 **he** i.e., Pedro

vey her from out her father's court according as she should give him direction; and also to make himself partaker of her journey and to wait upon her till she had seen the end of her determination.

Pedro, perceiving with what vehemency his lady and mistress had made request unto him, albeit he saw many perils and doubts depending in her pretense,[32] notwithstanding gave his consent to be at her disposition, promising her to further her with his best advice and to be ready to obey whatsoever she would please to command him. The match being thus agreed upon and all things prepared in a readiness for their departure, it happened there was a galley of Constantinople ready to depart, which Pedro, understanding, came to the captain, desiring him to have passage for himself and for a poor maid that was his sister which were bound to Constantinople upon certain urgent affairs. To which request the captain granted, willing him to prepare[33] aboard with all speed because the wind served him presently[34] to depart.

Pedro now coming to his mistress and telling her how he had handled the matter with the captain, she, liking very well of the device, disguising herself into very simple attire, stole away from out her father's court and came with Pedro—whom now she calleth brother—aboard the galley, where, all things being in readiness and the wind serving very well, they launched forth with their oars and set sail. When they were at the sea, the captain of the galley, taking the view of Silla, perceiving her singular beauty, he was better pleased in beholding of her face than in taking the height either of the sun or stars;* and thinking her by the homeliness of her apparel to be but some simple maiden, calling her into his cabin, he began to break[35] with her, after the sea fashion, desiring her to use his own cabin for her better ease, and during the time that she remained at the sea she should not want a bed; and then, whispering softly in her ear, he said that for want of a bedfellow he himself would supply that room. Silla, not being acquainted with any such talk, blushed for shame but made him no answer at all. My captain, feeling such a bickering within himself

32 **depending in her pretense** arising from her profession of purpose
33 **prepare** i.e., get ready, come   34 **presently** immediately   35 **break**
converse, declare his intention

the like whereof he had never endured upon the sea, was like[36] to be taken prisoner aboard his own ship and forced to yield himself a captive without any cannon shot; wherefore, to salve all sores and thinking it the readiest way to speed,[37] he began to break with Silla in the way of marriage, telling her how happy a voyage she had made to fall into the liking of such a one as himself was, who was able to keep and maintain her like a gentlewoman, and for her sake would likewise take her brother into his fellowship, whom he would by some means prefer[38] in such sort that both of them should have good cause to think themselves thrice happy—she to light of[39] such a husband, and he to light of such a brother. But Silla, nothing pleased with these preferments, desired him to cease his talk for that she did think herself indeed to be too unworthy such a one as he was; neither was she minded yet to marry, and therefore desired him to fix his fancy upon some that were better worthy than herself was and that could better like of his courtesy than she could do. The captain, seeing himself thus refused, being in a great chafe he said as followeth:

"Then, seeing you make so little account of my courtesy, proffered to one that is so far unworthy of it, from henceforth I will use the office of my authority. You shall know that I am the captain of this ship and have power to command and dispose of things at my pleasure; and seeing you have so scornfully rejected me to be your loyal husband, I will now take you by force and use you at my will, and so long as it shall please me will keep you for mine own store. There shall be no man able to defend you nor yet to persuade me from that[40] I have determined."

Silla, with these words being struck into a great fear, did think it now too late to rue her rash attempt, determined[41] rather to die with her own hands than to suffer herself to be abused in such sort. Therefore she most humbly desired the captain so much as he could to save her credit,[42] and saying that she must needs be at his will and disposition, that for that present he would depart and suffer[43] her till night, when in the dark he might take his pleasure without any

---

36 was like was about   **37 speed** succeed   **38 prefer** give advancement to   **39 light of** happen upon   **40 that** what   **41 determined** i.e., and determined   **42 credit** reputation   **43 suffer** excuse, indulge

manner of suspicion to the residue of his company. The captain, thinking now the goal to be more than half won, was contented so far to satisfy her request and departed out, leaving her alone in his cabin.

Silla, being alone by herself, drew out her knife, ready to strike herself to the heart, and, falling upon her knees, desired God to receive her soul as an acceptable sacrifice for her follies which she had so willfully committed, craving pardon for her sins and so forth, continuing a long and pitiful reconciliation to God, in the midst whereof there suddenly fell a wonderful storm, the terror whereof was such that there was no man but did think the seas would presently have swallowed them. The billows so suddenly arose with the rage of the wind that they were all glad to fall to[44] heaving out of water, for otherwise their feeble galley had never been able to have brooked[45] the seas. This storm continued all that day and the next night; and they, being driven to put room[46]* before the wind to keep the galley ahead the billow, were driven upon the main shore, where the galley brake all to pieces. There was every man providing to save his own life. Some gat upon hatches, boards, and casks, and were driven with the waves to and fro; but the greatest number were drowned, amongst the which Pedro was one. But Silla herself being in the cabin, as you have heard, took hold of a chest that was the captain's, the which, by the only providence of God, brought her safe to the shore. The which when she had recovered,[47] not knowing what was become of Pedro her man, she deemed that both he and all the rest had been drowned, for that she saw nobody upon the shore but herself. Wherefore, when she had awhile made great lamentations, complaining her mishaps, she began in the end to comfort herself with the hope that she had to see her Apollonius, and found such means that she brake open the chest that brought her to land, wherein she found good store of coin and sundry suits of apparel that were the captain's. And now, to prevent a number of injuries that might be proffered to a woman that was left in her case, she determined to leave her own apparel and to sort herself into some of those suits, that, being taken for a man, she might pass

---

44 fall to turn to   **45 brooked** endured   **46 room** sea room (? The original text reads "romer.")   **47 recovered** reached

through the country in the better safety. And as she changed her apparel she thought it likewise convenient to change her name, wherefore, not readily happening of any other, she called herself Silvio, by the name of her own brother, whom you have heard spoken of before.

In this manner she traveled to Constantinople, where she inquired out the palace of the Duke Apollonius; and thinking herself now to be both fit and able to play the servingman, she presented herself to the Duke, craving his service. The Duke, very willing to give succor unto strangers, perceiving him to be a proper smug[48] young man, gave him entertainment. Silla thought herself now more than satisfied for all the casualties that had happened unto her in her journey that she might at her pleasure take but the view of the Duke Apollonius, and above the rest of his servants was very diligent and attendant upon him, the which the Duke perceiving began likewise to grow into good liking with the diligence of his man, and therefore made him one of his chamber. Who but Silvio then was most near about him in helping of him to make him ready in a morning, in the setting of his ruffs, in the keeping of his chamber? Silvio pleased his master so well that above all the rest of his servants about him he had the greatest credit, and the Duke put him most in trust.

At this very instant there was remaining in the city a noble dame, a widow whose husband was but lately deceased, one of the noblest men that were in the parts of Grecia, who left his lady and wife large possessions and great livings. This lady's name was called Julina, who, besides the abundance of her wealth and the greatness of her revenues, had likewise the sovereignty of all the dames of Constantinople for her beauty. To this Lady Julina, Apollonius became an earnest suitor; and, according to the manner of wooers, besides fair words, sorrowful sighs, and piteous countenances, there must be sending of loving letters, chains, bracelets, brooches, rings, tablets, gems, jewels, and presents—I know not what. So my Duke, who in the time that he remained in the isle of Cyprus had no skill at all in the art of love although it were more than half proffered unto him, was now become a scholar in love's school and had already

48 **smug** spruce, trim

learned his first lesson: that is, to speak pitifully, to look ruthfully, to promise largely, to serve diligently, and to please carefully. Now he was learning his second lesson: that is, to reward liberally, to give bountifully, to present willingly, and to write lovingly. Thus Apollonius was so busied in his new study that I warrant you there was no man that could challenge him for playing the truant, he followed his profession with so good a will. And who must be the messenger to carry the tokens and love letters to the Lady Julina but Silvio, his man. In him the Duke reposed his only confidence to go between him and his lady.

Now, gentlewomen, do you think there could have been a greater torment devised wherewith to afflict the heart of Silla than herself to be made the instrument to work her own mishap, and to play the attorney in a cause that made so much against herself? But Silla, altogether desirous to please her master, cared nothing at all to offend herself, followed[49] his business with so good a will as if it had been in her own preferment.

Julina, now having many times taken the gaze of this young youth, Silvio, perceiving him to be of such excellent perfect grace, was so entangled with the often sight of this sweet temptation that she fell into as great a liking with the man as the master was with herself. And on a time Silvio being sent from his master with a message to the Lady Julina, as he began very earnestly to solicit in his master's behalf, Julina, interrupting him in his tale, said, "Silvio, it is enough that you have said for your master. From henceforth either speak for yourself or say nothing at all." Silla, abashed to hear these words, began in her mind to accuse the blindness of love, that Julina, neglecting the good will of so noble a duke, would prefer her love unto such a one as nature itself had denied to recompense her liking.

And now, for a time leaving matters depending[50] as you have heard, it fell out that the right Silvio indeed—whom you have heard spoken of before, the brother of Silla—was come to his father's court into the isle of Cyprus; where, understanding that his sister was departed in manner as you have heard, conjectured that the very occasion did pro-

---

49 followed i.e., and followed   **50 depending** pending, awaiting outcome

ceed of some liking had between Pedro her man that was missing with her and herself. But Silvio, who loved his sister as dearly as his own life, and the rather for that—as she was his natural sister, both by father and mother—so the one of them was so like the other in countenance and favor that there was no man able to discern the one from the other by their faces saving by their apparel, the one being a man, the other a woman.

Silvio therefore vowed to his father not only to seek out his sister Silla but also to revenge the villainy which he conceived in Pedro for the carrying away of his sister. And thus departing, having traveled through many cities and towns without hearing any manner of news of those he went to seek for, at the last he arrived at Constantinople, where, as he was walking in an evening for his own recreation on a pleasant green yard without[51] the walls of the city, he fortuned to meet with the Lady Julina, who likewise had been abroad to take the air. And as she suddenly cast her eyes upon Silvio, thinking him to be her old acquaintance—by reason they were so like one another, as you have heard before—said[52] unto him, "Sir Silvio, if your haste be not the greater, I pray you, let me have a little talk with you, seeing I have so luckily met you in this place."

Silvio, wondering to hear himself so rightly named, being but a stranger not of above two days' continuance in the city, very courteously came towards her, desirous to hear what she would say.

Julina, commanding her train something[53] to stand back, said as followeth: "Seeing my good will and friendly love hath been the only cause to make me so prodigal to offer that[54] I see is so lightly rejected, it maketh me to think that men be of this condition rather to desire those things which they cannot come by than to esteem or value of that which both largely and liberally is offered unto them. But if the liberality of my proffer hath made to seem less the value of the thing that I meant to present, it is but in your own conceit,[55] considering how many noble men there hath been here before, and be yet at this present, which hath both served, sued, and most humbly entreated to attain to that

---

51 without outside of **52 said** i.e., she said **53 something** somewhat
54 that what **55 conceit** conception

which to you of myself I have freely offered and, I perceive, is despised or at the least very lightly regarded."

Silvio, wondering at these words but more amazed that she could so rightly call him by his name, could not tell what to make of her speeches, assuring himself that she was deceived and did mistake him, did[56] think notwithstanding it had been a point of great simplicity[57] if he should forsake that which fortune had so favorably proffered unto him, perceiving by her train that she was some lady of great honor; and, viewing the perfection of her beauty and the excellency of her grace and countenance, did think it unpossible that she should be despised, and therefore answered thus:

"Madam, if before this time I have seemed to forget myself in neglecting your courtesy which so liberally you have meant[58] unto me, please it you to pardon what is past, and from this day forwards Silvio remaineth ready prest[59] to make such reasonable amends as his ability may any ways permit or as it shall please you to command."

Julina, the gladdest woman that might be to hear these joyful news, said, "Then, my Silvio, see you fail not tomorrow at night to sup with me at my own house, where I will discourse farther with you what amends you shall make me." To which request Silvio gave his glad consent, and thus they departed, very well pleased. And as Julina did think the time very long till she had reaped the fruit of her desire, so Silvio he[60] wished for harvest before corn could grow, thinking the time as long till he saw how matters would fall out. But, not knowing what lady she might be, he presently, before Julina was out of sight, demanded of one that was walking by what she was and how she was called, who satisfied Silvio in every point, and also in what part of the town her house did stand, whereby he might inquire it out.

Silvio, thus departing to his lodging, passed the night with very unquiet sleeps, and the next morning his mind ran so much of[61] his supper that he never cared neither for his breakfast nor dinner; and the day, to his seeming,

---

56 did i.e., he did   **57 simplicity** simplemindedness   **58 meant** intended to convey   **59 ready prest** ready and willing   **60 Silvio he** Silvio   **61 of** on

passed away so slowly that he had thought the stately steeds had been tired that draw the chariot of the sun, or else some other Joshua[62] had commanded them again to stand, and wished that Phaëthon[63] had been there with a whip.

Julina, on the other side, she had thought the clock setter had played the knave, the day came no faster forwards. But six o'clock being once strucken recovered comfort to both parties; and Silvio, hastening himself to the palace of Julina, where by her he was friendly welcomed and a sumptuous supper being made ready furnished with sundry sorts of delicate dishes, they sat them down, passing the suppertime with amorous looks, loving countenances, and secret glances conveyed from the one to the other, which did better satisfy them than the feeding of their dainty dishes.

Suppertime being thus spent, Julina did think it very unfitly[64] if she should turn Silvio to go seek his lodging in an evening, desired him therefore that he would take a bed in her house for that night; and, bringing him up into a fair chamber that was very richly furnished, she found such means that when all the rest of her household servants were abed and quiet, she came herself to bear Silvio company, where, concluding upon conditions that were in question between them, they passed the night with such joy and contentation[65] as might in that convenient time be wished for. But only[66] that Julina, feeding too much of some one dish above the rest, received a surfeit whereof she could not be cured in forty weeks after—a natural inclination in all women which are subject to longing and want[67] the reason to use a moderation in their diet. But, the morning approaching, Julina took her leave and conveyed herself into her own chamber; and when it was fair daylight, Silvio,* making himself ready, departed likewise about his affairs in the town, debating with himself how things had happened, being well assured that Julina had mistaken him; and therefore, for fear of further evils, determined to come no more there, but took his journey towards other places in

62 Joshua (For Joshua's commanding the sun to stand still, see Joshua 10:12–13.) **63 Phaëthon** son of the sun-god, destroyed by Jupiter in his rash attempt to steer the sun-god's chariot **64 unfitly** unsuitable, inappropriate **65 contentation** contentment **66 But only** except **67 want** lack

the parts of Grecia to see if he could learn any tidings of his sister Silla.

The Duke Apollonius, having made a long suit and never a whit the nearer of his purpose, came to Julina to crave her direct answer, either to accept of him and such conditions as he proffered unto her or else to give him his last farewell.

Julina, as you have heard, had taken an earnest-penny[68] of another, whom she* had thought had been Silvio, the Duke's man, was[69] at a controversy in herself what she might do. One while[70] she thought, seeing her occasion served so fit, to crave the Duke's good will for the marrying of his man; then again, she could not tell what displeasure the Duke would conceive, in that she should seem to prefer his man before himself, did[71] think it therefore best to conceal the matter till she might speak with Silvio, to use his opinion how these matters should be handled; and hereupon resolving herself, desiring the Duke to pardon her speeches, said as followeth:

"Sir Duke, for that from this time forwards I am no longer of myself, having given my full power and authority over to another whose wife I now remain by faithful vow and promise, and albeit I know the world will wonder when they shall understand the fondness[72] of my choice, yet I trust you yourself will nothing dislike with me, sith[73] I have meant no other thing than the satisfying of mine own contentation and liking."

The Duke, hearing these words, answered: "Madam, I must then content myself, although against my will, having the law in your own hands to like of whom you list and to make choice where it pleaseth you."

Julina, giving the Duke great thanks that would content himself with such patience, desired him likewise to give his free consent and good will to the party whom she had chosen to be her husband.

"Nay, surely, madam," quoth the Duke, "I will never give my consent that any other man shall enjoy you than myself. I have made too great account of you than so lightly to pass you away with my good will. But seeing it lieth not in me to

---

68 earnest-penny small sum paid in earnest to secure a bargain   **69 was** i.e., and she was   **70 One while** on the one hand   **71 did** i.e., and did
72 fondness foolishness   **73 nothing dislike with me, sith** take no dislike to me, since

let[74] you, having, as you say, made your own choice, so from henceforwards I leave you to your own liking, always willing you well, and thus will take my leave."

The Duke departed towards his own house, very sorrowful that Julina had thus served him. But in the mean space[75] that the Duke had remained in the house of Julina, some of his servants fell into talk and conference with the servants of Julina, where, debating between them of the likelihood of the marriage between the Duke and the lady, one of the servants of Julina said that he never saw his lady and mistress use so good countenance to the Duke himself as she had done to Silvio his man, and began to report with what familiarity and courtesy she had received him, feasted him, and lodged him, and that in his opinion Silvio was like to speed[76] before the Duke or any other that were suitors.

This tale was quickly brought to the Duke himself, who, making better inquiry in the matter, found it to be true that was reported; and, better considering of the words which Julina had used towards himself, was very well assured that it could be no other than his own man that had thrust his nose so far out of joint. Wherefore, without any further respect,[77] caused[78] him to be thrust into a dungeon, where he was kept prisoner in a very pitiful plight.

Poor Silvio, having got intelligence by some of his fellows what was the cause that the Duke his master did bear such displeasure unto him, devised all the means he could, as well by mediation* by his fellows as otherwise by petitions and supplications to the Duke, that he would suspend his judgment till perfect proof were had in the matter, and then, if any manner of thing did fall out against him whereby the Duke had cause to take any grief, he would confess himself worthy not only of imprisonment but also of most vile and shameful death. With these petitions he daily plied the Duke, but all in vain, for the Duke thought he had made so good proof that he was thoroughly confirmed in his opinion against his man.

But the Lady Julina, wondering what made Silvio that he was so slack in his visitation and why he absented himself so long from her presence, began to think that all was not

---

74 let hinder **75 space** time **76 like to speed** likely to succeed
77 respect consideration **78 caused** i.e., he caused

well. But in the end, perceiving no decoction[79] of her former surfeit—received as you have heard—and finding in herself an unwonted swelling in her belly, assuring herself to be with child, fearing to become quite bankrupt of her honor, did think it more than time to seek out a father, and made such secret search and diligent inquiry that she learned the truth how Silvio was kept in prison by the Duke his master. And minding[80] to find a present remedy, as well for the love she bare[81] to Silvio as for the maintenance of her credit and estimation, she speedily hasted to the palace of the Duke, to whom she said as followeth:

"Sir Duke, it may be that you will think my coming to your house in this sort doth something[82] pass the limits of modesty, the which, I protest before God, proceedeth of this desire that the world should know how justly I seek means to maintain my honor. But to the end I seem not tedious with prolixity of words, nor to use other than direct circumstances, know, sir, that the love I bear to my only beloved Silvio, whom I do esteem more than all the jewels in the world, whose personage I regard more than my own life, is the only cause of my attempted journey, beseeching you that all the whole displeasure which I understand you have conceived against him may be imputed unto my charge, and that it would please you lovingly to deal with him whom of myself I have chosen rather for the satisfaction of mine honest liking than for the vain preeminences or honorable dignities looked after[83] by ambitious minds."

The Duke, having heard this discourse, caused Silvio presently[84] to be sent for and to be brought before him, to whom he said: "Had it not been sufficient for thee, when I had reposed[85] myself in thy fidelity and the trustiness of thy service, that thou shouldst so traitorously deal with me, but since that time hast not spared still to abuse me with so many forgeries and perjured protestations, not only hateful unto me, whose simplicity thou thinkest to be such that by the plot of thy pleasant tongue thou wouldst make me believe a manifest untruth, but most abominable be thy doings in the presence and sight of God, that hast[86] not spared to blaspheme his holy name by calling him to be a witness

79 decoction diminishing 80 minding intending 81 bare bore
82 something somewhat 83 looked after sought after 84 presently
immediately 85 reposed entrusted 86 that hast (you) who have

to maintain thy leasings,[87] and so detestably wouldst forswear thyself in a matter that is so openly known."

Poor Silvio, whose innocency was such that he might lawfully swear, seeing Julina to be there in place, answered thus:

"Most noble Duke, well understanding your conceived grief, most humbly I beseech you patiently to hear my excuse, not minding[88] thereby to aggravate or heap up your wrath and displeasure, protesting before God that there is nothing in the world which I regard so much or do esteem so dear as your good grace and favor, but desirous that Your Grace should know my innocency, and to clear myself of such impositions[89] wherewith I know I am wrongfully accused; which, as I understand, should be in the practicing[90] of the Lady Julina, who standeth here in place, whose acquittance for my better discharge[91] now I most humbly crave, protesting before the almighty God that neither in thought, word, nor deed I have not otherwise used myself than according to the bond and duty of a servant that is both willing and desirous to further his master's suits; which if I have otherwise said than that is true, you, Madam Julina, who can very well decide the depths of all this doubt, I most humbly beseech you to certify a truth if I have in anything missaid or have otherwise spoken than is right and just."

Julina, having heard this discourse which Silvio had made, perceiving that he stood in great awe of the Duke's displeasure, answered thus: "Think not, my Silvio, that my coming hither is to accuse you of any misdemeanor towards your master, so I do not deny but[92] in all such embassages wherein towards me you have been employed you have used the office of a faithful and trusty messenger. Neither am I ashamed to confess that the first day that mine eyes did behold the singular behavior, the notable courtesy, and other innumerable gifts wherewith my Silvio is endowed, but that beyond all measure my heart was so inflamed that impossible it was for me to quench the fervent love or extinguish the least part of my conceived torment before I had bewrayed[93] the same unto him and of my own motion craved

87 leasings lies   **88 minding** intending   **89 impositions** accusations
90 practicing devising   **91 discharge** clearing of blame   **92 so . . . but**
and so I do not deny but that   **93 bewrayed** revealed

his promised faith and loyalty of marriage. And now is the time to manifest the same unto the world which hath been done before God and between ourselves, knowing that it is not needful to keep secret that which is neither evil done nor hurtful to any person. Therefore, as I said before, Silvio is my husband by plighted faith, whom I hope to obtain without offense or displeasure of anyone, trusting that there is no man that will so far forget himself as to restrain that which God hath left at liberty for every wight,[94] or that will seek by cruelty to force ladies to marry otherwise than according to their own liking. Fear not then, my Silvio, to keep your faith and promise which you have made unto me; and as for the rest, I doubt not things will so fall out as you shall have no manner of cause to complain."

Silvio, amazed to hear these words, for that Julina by her speech seemed to confirm that which he most of all desired to be quit of,[95] said: "Who would have thought that a lady of so great honor and reputation would herself be the ambassador of a thing so prejudicial and uncomely for her estate! What plighted promises be these which be spoken of? Altogether ignorant unto me, which, if it be otherwise than I have said, you, sacred goddess, consume me straight with flashing flames of fire! But what words might I use to give credit to the truth and innocency of my cause? Ah, Madam Julina! I desire no other testimony than your own honesty and virtue, thinking that you will not so much blemish the brightness of your honor, knowing that a woman is or should be the image of courtesy, continency, and shame-fastness—from the which, so soon as she stoopeth and leaveth the office of her duty and modesty, besides the degradation of her honor, she thrusteth herself into the pit of perpetual infamy. And as I cannot think you would so far forget yourself by the refusal of a noble duke to dim the light of your renown and glory, which hitherto you have maintained amongst the best and noblest ladies, by such a one as I know myself to be, too far unworthy your degree and calling, so most humbly I beseech you to confess a truth whereto tendeth those vows and promises you speak of—which speeches be so obscure unto me as I know not for my life how I might understand them."

94 wight person   **95 quit of** acquitted of

Julina, something nipped with[96] these speeches, said: "And what is the matter, that now you make so little account of your Julina? That, being my husband indeed, have the face to deny me to whom thou art contracted by so many solemn oaths? What? Art thou ashamed to have me to thy wife? How much oughtst thou rather to be ashamed to break thy promised faith and to have[97] despised the holy and dreadful name of God? But that time[98] constraineth me to lay open[99] that which shame rather willeth I should dissemble and keep secret. Behold me then here, Silvio, whom thou has gotten with child; who, if thou be of such honesty as I trust for all this[100] I shall find, then the thing is done without prejudice or any hurt to my conscience, considering that by the professed faith[101] thou didst account me for thy wife and I received thee for my spouse and loyal husband, swearing by the almighty God that no other than you have made the conquest and triumph of my chastity, whereof I crave no other witness than yourself and mine own conscience."

I pray you, gentlewomen, was not this a foul oversight of Julina, that would so precisely swear so great an oath that she was gotten with child by one that was altogether unfurnished with implements for such a turn? For God's love take heed, and let this be an example to you when you be with child how you swear who is the father before you have had good proof and knowledge of the party; for men be so subtle and full of sleight that, God knows, a woman may quickly be deceived.

But now to return to our Silvio, who, hearing an oath sworn so divinely that he had gotten a woman with child, was like to believe[102] that it had been true in very deed; but, remembering his own impediment, thought it impossible that he should commit such an act and therefore, half in a chafe,[103] he said:

"What law is able to restrain the foolish indiscretion of a woman that yieldeth herself to her own desires? What shame is able to bridle or withdraw her from her mind and

96 something nipped with somewhat taken aback by   97 have cause to be   98 that time i.e., the time of my pregnancy   99 lay open reveal   100 for all this despite all this (denial)   101 the professed faith the faith we all profess   102 like to believe near to believing   103 in a chafe angry

madness, or with what snaffle is it possible to hold her back
from the execution of her filthiness? But what abomination
is this, that a lady of such a house should so forget the
greatness of her estate, the alliance whereof she is de-
scended, the nobility of her deceased husband, and maketh
no conscience to shame and slander herself with such a one
as I am, being so far unfit and unseemly for her degree! But
how horrible is it to hear the name of God so defaced that
we make no more account, but for the maintenance of our
mischiefs we fear no whit at all to forswear his holy name,
as though he were not in all his dealings most righteous,
true, and just, and will not only lay open our leasings[104] to
the world but will likewise punish the same with most
sharp and bitter scourges."

Julina, not able to endure him to proceed any farther in
his sermon, was already surprised with a vehement grief,
began bitterly to cry out, uttering these speeches following:

"Alas! Is it possible that the sovereign justice of God can
abide a mischief so great and cursed? Why may I not now
suffer death rather than the infamy which I see to wander
before mine eyes? Oh, happy, and more than right happy,
had I been if inconstant Fortune had not devised this treason wherein I am surprised and caught! Am I thus become
to be entangled with snares and in the hands of him who,
enjoying the spoils of my honor, will openly deprive me of
my fame by making me a common fable to all posterity in
time to come? Ah, traitor and discourteous wretch! Is this
the recompense of the honest and firm amity which I have
borne thee? Wherein have I deserved this discourtesy? By
loving thee more than thou art able to deserve? Is it I, arrant thief, is it I upon whom thou thinkest to work thy mischiefs? Dost thou think me no better worth but that thou
mayst prodigally waste my honor at thy pleasure? Didst
thou dare to adventure upon me, having my conscience
wounded with so deadly a treason? Ah, unhappy and above
all other most unhappy, that have so charily[105] preserved
mine honor and now am made a prey to satisfy a young
man's lust that hath coveted nothing but the spoil of my
chastity and good name!"

104 leasings lies   **105 charily** carefully, frugally

Herewithal her tears so gushed down her cheeks that she was not able to open her mouth to use any farther speech.

The Duke, who stood by all this while and heard this whole discourse, was wonderfully moved with compassion towards Julina, knowing that from her infancy she had ever so honorably used herself that there was no man able to detect her of[106] any misdemeanor otherwise than beseemed a lady of her estate. Wherefore, being fully resolved that Silvio, his man, had committed this villainy against her, in a great fury, drawing his rapier, he said unto Silvio:

"How canst thou, arrant thief, show thyself so cruel and careless to such as do thee honor? Hast thou so little regard of such a noble lady as humbleth herself to such a villain as thou art, who, without any respect either of her renown or noble estate, canst be content to seek the wrack and utter ruin of her honor? But frame[107] thyself to make such satisfaction as she requireth—although I know, unworthy wretch, that thou art not able to make her the least part of amends—or I swear by God that thou shalt not escape the death which I will minister to thee with my own hands. And therefore advise thee well what thou dost."

Silvio, having heard this sharp sentence, fell down on his knees before the Duke, craving for mercy, desiring that he might be suffered to speak with the Lady Julina apart, promising to satisfy her according to her own contentation.[108]

"Well," quoth the Duke, "I take thy word; and therewithal I advise thee that thou perform thy promise, or otherwise I protest, before God, I will make thee such an example to the world that all traitors shall tremble for fear how they do seek the dishonoring of ladies."

But now Julina had conceived so great grief against Silvio that there was much ado to persuade her to talk with him. But remembering her own case, desirous to hear what excuse he could make, in the end she agreed, and, being brought into a place severally[109] by themselves, Silvio began with a piteous voice to say as followeth:

"I know not, madam, of whom I might make complaint, whether of you or of myself, or rather of Fortune, which

106 of in **107 frame** prepare **108 to her own contentation** to her heart's content **109 severally** separately

hath conducted and brought us both into so great adversity. I see that you receive great wrong, and I am condemned against all right; you in peril to abide the bruit[110] of spiteful tongues, and I in danger to lose the thing that I most desire. And although I could allege many reasons to prove my sayings true, yet I refer myself to the experience and bounty of your mind." And herewithal loosing his garments down to his stomach, and showed Julina his breasts and pretty teats surmounting far the whiteness of snow itself, saying: "Lo, madam! Behold here the party whom you have challenged to be the father of your child. See, I am a woman, the daughter of a noble duke, who, only for the love of him whom you so lightly have shaken off, have forsaken my father, abandoned my country, and, in manner as you see, am become a servingman, satisfying myself but with the only[111] sight of my Apollonius. And now, madam, if my passion were not vehement and my torments without comparison, I would wish that my feigned griefs might be laughed to scorn and my dissembled pains to be rewarded with flouts. But my love being pure, my travail[112] continual, and my griefs endless, I trust, madam, you will not only excuse me of crime but also pity my distress, the which, I protest, I would still have kept secret if my fortune would so have permitted."

Julina did now think herself to be in a worse case than ever she was before, for now she knew not whom to challenge to be the father of her child; wherefore, when she had told the Duke the very certainty of the discourse which Silvio had made unto her, she departed to her own house with such grief and sorrow that she purposed never to come out of her own doors again alive to be a wonder and mocking stock to the world.

But the Duke, more amazed to hear this strange discourse of Silvio, came unto him, whom, when he had viewed with better consideration, perceived indeed that it was Silla, the daughter of Duke Pontus, and embracing her in his arms he said:

"Oh, the branch of all virtue and the flower of courtesy itself! Pardon me, I beseech you, of all such discourtesies as I have ignorantly committed towards you, desiring you that

110 bruit clamor　**111 but with the only** only with the　**112 travail** hardship

without farther memory of ancient griefs you will accept of me, who is more joyful and better contented with your presence than if the whole world were at my commandment. Where hath there ever been found such liberality in a lover which, having been trained up and nourished amongst the delicacies and banquets of the court, accompanied with trains of many fair and noble ladies, living in pleasure and in the midst of delights, would so prodigally adventure yourself, neither fearing mishaps nor misliking to take such pains as I know you have not been accustomed unto? O liberality never heard of before! O fact that can never be sufficiently rewarded! O true love most pure and unfeigned!" Herewithal sending for the most artificial workmen,[113] he provided for her sundry suits of sumptuous apparel, and the marriage day appointed, which was celebrated with great triumph through the whole city of Constantinople, everyone praising the nobleness of the Duke. But so many as did behold the excellent beauty of Silla gave her the praise above all the rest of the ladies in the troop.

The matter seemed so wonderful and strange that the bruit[114] was spread throughout all the parts of Grecia, insomuch that it came to the hearing of Silvio, who, as you have heard, remained in those parts to inquire of his sister. He, being the gladdest man in the world, hasted to Constantinople where, coming to his sister, he was joyfully received and most lovingly welcomed and entertained of the Duke his brother-in-law. After he had remained there two or three days, the Duke revealed unto Silvio the whole discourse how it happened between his sister and the Lady Julina, and how his sister was challenged for getting a woman with child. Silvio, blushing with these words, was stricken with great remorse to make Julina amends, understanding her to be a noble lady and was left defamed to the world through his default.[115] He therefore bewrayed[116] the whole circumstance to the Duke, whereof the Duke, being very joyful, immediately repaired[117] with Silvio to the house of Julina, whom they found in her chamber in great lamentation and mourning. To whom the Duke said: "Take courage, madam,

---

113 **artificial workmen** craftsmen skilled in their art   114 **bruit** rumor
115 **default** fault   116 **bewrayed** revealed   117 **repaired** went

for behold here a gentleman that will not stick[118] both to father your child and to take you for his wife; no inferior person, but the son and heir of a noble duke, worthy of your estate and dignity."

Julina, seeing Silvio in place, did know very well that he was the father of her child and was so ravished with joy that she knew not whether she were awake or in some dream. Silvio, embracing her in his arms, craving forgiveness of all that was past, concluded[119] with her the marriage day, which was presently accomplished with great joy and contentation to all parties. And thus, Silvio having attained a noble wife, and Silla, his sister, her desired husband, they passed the residue of their days with such delight as those that have accomplished the perfection of their felicities.

———————

The text is based on Barnabe Riche, *Riche His Farewell to Military Profession*, London, 1581.

The following indicate changes in the original text.

p. 98 *sip soope   p. 102 *stars Starre   p. 104 *room romer   p. 109 *Silvio Silvano
p. 110 *she he   p. 111 *mediation meditation

———————

118 stick hesitate   119 concluded settled

Further Reading

Auden, W. H. "Music in Shakespeare." *"The Dyer's Hand" and Other Essays*. New York: Random House, 1948. Auden finds dark tones disturbing the comedy of *Twelfth Night*. Viola and Antonio are characters whose desires are too strong to be contained by the play's comic conventions. The songs, Auden argues, express the play's complex comic feeling: by themselves they are beautiful, but located within the psychological matrix of the play they are cruel, selfish, and self-indulgent.

Barber, C. L. "Testing Courtesy and Humanity in *Twelfth Night*." *Shakespeare's Festive Comedy*. Princeton, N.J.: Princeton Univ. Press, 1959. Focusing on the relation of the dramatic form to the social forms of Elizabethan holidays, Barber examines the Saturnalian patterns in Shakespearean comedy. In *Twelfth Night*, the reversal of sexual and social roles permits both characters and audiences to move, in Barber's phrase, "through release to clarification," as characters (with the telling exception of the puritanical Malvolio), caught up in delusions and misapprehensions, ultimately discover freedom, love, and self-knowledge through the festive action.

Barton, Anne. "*As You Like It* and *Twelfth Night:* Shakespeare's Sense of an Ending." In *Shakespearian Comedy*, ed. Malcolm Bradbury and D. J. Palmer. Stratford-upon-Avon Studies 14. London: Edward Arnold, 1972. Except for Malvolio, Barton argues, all characters and the audience participate in the play's festivity, but she finds the play's harmonies to be elusive and fragile: the improbable romantic world of escape, disguise, and irrational love is announced as a triumph of art, and Feste's final song gently leads us out of the golden world of fiction back to our imperfect world of fact.

Brown, John Russell. "Directions for *Twelfth Night, or What You Will*." *Tulane Drama Review* 5, no. 4 (1961): 77–88. Rpt. in *Shakespeare's Plays in Performance*. New York: St. Martin's Press, 1967. Brown surveys *Twelfth Night* on the stage in the 1950s to reveal the multiplicity of dramatic interpretations that it permits and to suggest the possibility of a production fully responsive to the play's range and complexity. He offers his own solution to the visual problems that *Twelfth Night* poses as an example of one way in which a director might use available theatrical resources to respond to the demands made by the unity and the imaginative power of the text.

Hartwig, Joan. "*Twelfth Night* and Parodic Subplot." *Shakespeare's Analogical Scene*. Lincoln, Neb.: Univ. of Nebraska Press, 1983. Finding the play to be concerned with the conflict between individual will and a design beyond human control, Hartwig considers the relation of the play's two plots. Only Malvolio's fate is determined by acts of human will, and the lack of forgiveness at his exit points to the central difference between the plots: the subplot is motivated by revenge, a human act that fragments and destroys; the main plot is directed by love, the concern of some benevolent higher agency, which creates and directs the play's harmonies.

Hollander, John. "*Twelfth Night* and the Morality of Indulgence." *Sewanee Review* 67 (1959): 220–238. Rpt. in *Discussions of Shakespeare's Romantic Comedy*, ed. Herbert Weil, Jr. Boston: D. C. Heath, 1966; and in *Essays in Shakespearean Criticism*, ed. James L. Calderwood and Harold E. Toliver. Englewood Cliffs, N.J.: Prentice-Hall, 1970. Arguing that in its use of a fully dramatized metaphor (of feasting and satiety) the play rejects the comic model provided by Ben Jonson (the characteristically static comedy of humors), Hollander sees *Twelfth Night* as a comedy of emotional and moral purgation in which excessive appetite is corrected through its indulgence. Except in the case of Malvolio, indulgence succeeds in releasing the fully human self from the limitations of comic stereotype.

Howard, Jean E. "The Orchestration of *Twelfth Night*: The Rhythm of Restraint and Release." *Shakespeare's Art of Orchestration: Stage Technique and Audience Response*. Urbana and Chicago: Univ. of Illinois Press, 1984. Howard considers how Shakespeare orchestrates an audience's experience of the play. The inadequacy of the characters' emotional postures is revealed through their inhibiting effects on the play's action and language. The audience's desire for the generosity and joy that has been frustrated is finally satisfied by the recognitions of the ending.

Jenkins, Harold. "Shakespeare's *Twelfth Night.*" *Rice Institute Pamphlets* 45 (1959): 19–42. Rpt. in *Shakespeare, the Comedies: A Collection of Critical Essays,* ed. Kenneth Muir. Englewood Cliffs, N.J.: Prentice-Hall, 1965. Identifying *Twelfth Night*'s most important source as Shakespeare's own *The Comedy of Errors* and *The Two Gentlemen of Verona,* Jenkins examines the play's deepening of the emotional patterns of the earlier plays. The genuineness of Viola's feeling serves not only to measure the emotions of others but also to release both Orsino and Olivia from their self-indulgence, a movement that finds an ironic echo in the subplot as Malvolio remains locked in his self-love.

Kermode, Frank. "The Mature Comedies." In *Early Shakespeare,* ed. John Russell Brown and Bernard Harris. Stratford-upon-Avon Studies 3. London: Edward Arnold, 1961. In an essay seeking to characterize the achievement of the mature comedies, Kermode considers *Twelfth Night* in relation to two aspects of the Twelfth Night celebrations: its licensing of misrule and the confounding of identity and authority. The play's comic confusions and misapprehensions reflect the festive pattern, moving from a superficial comedy of errors to a complex and sophisticated comedy of identity.

King, Walter N., ed. *Twentieth Century Interpretations of "Twelfth Night."* Englewood Cliffs, N.J.: Prentice-Hall, 1968. King's introductory essay to this collection of criticism considers the collision of perspectives in *Twelfth Night,* and his selection of essays is designed to demonstrate the variety of critical approaches that it permits. King includes studies by Sylvan Barnet, H. B. Charlton, Alan Downer, and Leslie Hotson, as well as essays, considered here, by Barber, Hollander, Leech, Salingar, and Summers.

Leech, Clifford. "*Twelfth Night,* or What Delights You." *"Twelfth Night" and Shakespearian Comedy.* Toronto: Univ. of Toronto Press, 1965. *Twelfth Night,* according to Leech, tempers its harmonies with the awareness of the contrivance needed to produce them. The play is never harsh, Leech finds, but the precariousness of the comic triumph is evident—in our discomfort at Malvolio's humiliation, in the poignancy of Antonio's relationship with Sebastian, in the complicated sexual awareness produced by boy actors playing women disguised as men, and in the refusal of the ending fully to credit the imminent marriages.

Leggatt, Alexander. *"Twelfth Night." Shakespeare's Comedy of Love.* London: Methuen, 1974. Leggatt examines *Twelfth Night*'s emphasis upon individuals isolated by nature or circumstance. The play dramatizes the difficulties of forming relationships, and significantly, Leggatt finds, it ends not with a dance or procession of lovers but with the solitary figure of Feste. The love plot is resolved happily, but its resolution depends upon formal organization rather than upon psychological growth, revealing the tension between conventional and realistic art.

Lewalski, Barbara K. "Thematic Patterns in *Twelfth Night.*" *Shakespeare Studies* 1 (1965): 168–181. Lewalski considers the religious dimension of *Twelfth Night*, exploring the significance of the play's title (Twelfth Night celebrates the journey of the Magi to Bethlehem and is observed on the twelfth and final day of the Christmas season, January 6). The play, Lewalski argues, is not an allegory of Christ's action in the world but a secular analogue of it: Sebastian and Viola bring peace and love to a disordered world, though Feste's final song reminds us that the real world is less easily perfected than the comic universe of the play.

Nevo, Ruth. "Nature's Bias." *Comic Transformations in Shakespeare.* London and New York: Methuen, 1980. Nevo regards *Twelfth Night* as Shakespeare's most brilliant realization of the possibilities of a dramatic form that is at once comic and corrective. The play enacts and exorcises characters' fantasies and obsessions. Nevo explores the gentle masculinity of Sebastian in this process, whose presence permits the joyful recognitions and remedies of the end.

Palmer, D. J. *Shakespeare, "Twelfth Night": A Casebook.* London: Macmillan, 1972. Palmer's introduction to this collection of critical commentary discusses the subtle play of lyrical and dissonant notes in *Twelfth Night* and usefully surveys the play's occasion, date, and sources as well as the history of criticism that it has provoked. The selections that he offers partially trace this history, from seventeenth-century comments on the play to the work of twentieth-century critics such as Barber, Bradley, Charlton, and Hotson.

Salingar, Leo G. "The Design of *Twelfth Night.*" *Shakespeare Quarterly* 9 (1958): 117–139. Rpt. in *Discussions of Shakespeare's Romantic Comedy*, ed. Herbert Weil, Jr. Boston: D. C. Heath, 1966. Salingar examines Shakespeare's transformation of classical and Renaissance romance materials into a comedy of misrule exploring the psychology of love. The narrative and emotional improbabilities of the sources are used to reveal love's folly as well as its life-affirming power. *Twelfth Night* presents and interrogates this paradoxical conception of love, as self-deception gives way to mistaken identities sorted out by the action of a fate responsive to human desire.

Summers, Joseph H. "The Masks of *Twelfth Night.*" *University Review of Kansas City* 22 (1955): 25–32. Rpt. in *Discussions of Shakespeare's Romantic Comedy*, ed. Herbert Weil, Jr. Boston: D. C. Heath, 1966; and in *Shakespeare: Modern Essays in Criticism*, ed. Leonard F. Dean. Rev. ed., London, Oxford, and New York: Oxford Univ. Press, 1967. *Twelfth Night*, according to Summers, in its elaborate dance of maskers enacts their pursuit of self-knowledge and happiness. Everyone wears a mask, and, in general, we laugh *with* those who are aware of and in control of the roles they play, and we laugh *at* those who are not. The clown, Feste—the one professional in the business of masking—is able to unmask the pretensions of others, even revealing the mask of the play itself to be only a fiction of an idealized world.

Welsford, Enid. *The Fool: His Social and Literary History.* Esp. pp. 251–252. London: Faber and Faber, 1935. In her study of the literary and social history of the Fool, Welsford considers Feste as a lord of misrule presiding over the festivities of *Twelfth Night.* His wit gives unity to the play's action, focusing its values. Appropriately he is given the play's final word, dissolving the fiction into a song that points to harsher realities than the comedy would admit.

Memorable Lines

If music be the food of love, play on. (ORSINO 1.1.1)

And what should I do in Illyria? (VIOLA 1.2.3)

Care's an enemy to life. (SIR TOBY 1.3.2–3)

I am a great eater of beef, and I believe that does harm to my wit. (SIR ANDREW 1.3.84–85)

God give them wisdom that have it; and those that are fools, let them use their talents. (FESTE 1.5.14–15)

As there is no true cuckold but calamity, so beauty's a flower. (FESTE 1.5.48–49)

I wear not motley in my brain. (FESTE 1.5.53–54)

You do usurp yourself; for what is yours to bestow is not yours to reserve. (VIOLA 1.5.183–184)

Lady, you are the cruel'st she alive
If you will lead these graces to the grave
And leave the world no copy. (VIOLA 1.5.236–238)

[*Song*] O mistress mine, where are you roaming? (FESTE 2.3.39)

[*Song*] What is love? 'tis not hereafter;
Present mirth hath present laughter;
  What's to come is still unsure.
In delay there lies no plenty,
Then come kiss me, sweet and twenty;
  Youth's a stuff will not endure. (FESTE 2.3.47–52)

Dost thou think, because thou art virtuous, there shall be no more cakes and ale? (SIR TOBY 2.3.114–115)

We men may say more, swear more, but indeed
Our shows are more than will; for still we prove
Much in our vows, but little in our love.

(VIOLA 2.4.116–118)

I am all the daughters of my father's house,
And all the brothers too. (VIOLA 2.4.120–121)

'Tis but fortune, all is fortune. (MALVOLIO 2.5.23)

Be not afraid of greatness. Some are born great, some
achieve greatness, and some have greatness thrust upon 'em.

(*Letter* 2.5.141–143)

Remember who commended thy yellow stockings, and
wished to see thee ever cross-gartered.

(*Letter* 2.5.149–151)

This fellow is wise enough to play the fool,
And to do that well craves a kind of wit. (VIOLA 3.1.60–61)

Then westward ho! (VIOLA 3.1.134)

This is very midsummer madness. (OLIVIA 3.4.58)

Thus the whirligig of time brings in his revenges.

(FESTE 5.1.376–377)

I'll be revenged on the whole pack of you!

(MALVOLIO 5.1.378)

He hath been most notoriously abused. (OLIVIA 5.1.379)

[*Song*]   When that I was and a little tiny boy,
   With hey, ho, the wind and the rain,
A foolish thing was but a toy,
   For the rain it raineth every day. (FESTE 5.1.389–392)

Contributors

DAVID BEVINGTON, Phyllis Fay Horton Professor of Humanities at the University of Chicago, is editor of *The Complete Works of Shakespeare* (Scott, Foresman, 1980) and of *Medieval Drama* (Houghton Mifflin, 1975). His latest critical study is *Action Is Eloquence: Shakespeare's Language of Gesture* (Harvard University Press, 1984).

DAVID SCOTT KASTAN, Professor of English and Comparative Literature at Columbia University, is the author of *Shakespeare and the Shapes of Time* (University Press of New England, 1982).

JAMES HAMMERSMITH, Associate Professor of English at Auburn University, has published essays on various facets of Renaissance drama, including literary criticism, textual criticism, and printing history.

ROBERT KEAN TURNER, Professor of English at the University of Wisconsin–Milwaukee, is a general editor of the New Variorum Shakespeare (Modern Language Association of America) and a contributing editor to *The Dramatic Works in the Beaumont and Fletcher Canon* (Cambridge University Press, 1966–).

JAMES SHAPIRO, who coedited the bibliographies with David Scott Kastan, is Assistant Professor of English at Columbia University.

✣

JOSEPH PAPP, one of the most important forces in theater today, is the founder and producer of the New York Shakespeare Festival, America's largest and most prolific theatrical institution. Since 1954 Mr. Papp has produced or directed all but one of Shakespeare's plays—in Central Park, in schools, off and on Broadway, and at the Festival's permanent home, The Public Theater. He has also produced such award-winning plays and musical works as *Hair, A Chorus Line, Plenty,* and *The Mystery of Edwin Drood,* among many others.